# HAMLET

## WILLIAM SHAKESPEARE

*(handwritten annotations):* young Hamlets (Hamlets king) young king, uncle, Hamlets Bro

m. Queen Gertrude — King Claudius

~~King Hamlet~~

Prince/young Hamlet

# CONTENTS

# DRAMATIS PERSONÆ

CLAUDIUS, king of Denmark.

HAMLET, son to the late, and nephew to the present king.

POLONIUS, lord chamberlain.

HORATIO, friend to Hamlet.

LAERTES, son to Polonius.

VOLTIMAND,

CORNELIUS,

ROSENCRANTZ,

GUILDENSTERN,

OSRIC,

A Gentleman,

A Priest.

MARCELLUS,

BERNARDO,

FRANCISCO, a soldier.

REYNALDO, servant to Polonius.

Players.

Two Clowns, grave-diggers.

FORTINBRAS, prince of Norway.

A Captain.

English Ambassadors.

GERTRUDE, queen of Denmark, and mother to Hamlet.

OPHELIA, daughter to Polonius.

Lords, Ladies, Officers, Soldiers, Sailors, Messengers, and other Attendants.

Ghost of Hamlet's Father.
*SCENE:* Denmark

# ACT I

SCENE I. ELSINORE. A PLATFORM BEFORE THE CASTLE.

(*FRANCISCO at his post. Enter to him BERNARDO.*)

*BER.* Who's there?
*FRAN.* Nay, answer me: stand, and unfold yourself.
*BER.* Long live the king!
*FRAN.* Bernardo?
*BER.* He. 5
*FRAN.* You come most carefully upon your hour.
*BER.* 'Tis now struck twelve; get thee to bed, Francisco.
*FRAN.* For this relief much thanks: 'tis bitter cold, And I am sick at heart.
*BER.* Have you had quiet guard?
*FRAN.* Not a mouse stirring. 10
*BER.* Well, good night.
If you do meet Horatio and Marcellus,
The rivals of my watch, bid them make haste.
*FRAN.* I think I hear them. Stand, ho! Who is there?

(*ENTER HORATIO AND MARCELLUS.*)

*HOR.* Friends to this ground.
*MAR.* And liegemen to the Dane. 15
*FRAN.* Give you good night.

*MAR.* O, farewell, honest soldier:
Who hath relieved you?
*FRAN.* Bernardo hath my place.
Give you good night. *(Exit.)*
*MAR.* Holla! Bernardo!
*BER.* Say,
What, is Horatio there?
*HOR.* A piece of him.
*BER.* Welcome, Horatio: welcome, good Marcellus.

*MAR.* 20 What, has this thing appear'd again to-night?
*BER.* I have seen nothing.
*MAR.* Horatio says 'tis but our fantasy,
And will not let belief take hold of him
Touching this dreaded sight, twice seen of us: 25
Therefore I have entreated him along
With us to watch the minutes of this night,
That if again this apparition come,
He may approve our eyes and speak to it.
*HOR.* Tush, tush, 'twill not appear.
*BER.* Sit down awhile; 30
And let us once again assail your ears,
That are so fortified against our story,
What we have two nights seen.
*HOR.* Well, sit we down,
And let us hear Bernardo speak of this.
*BER.* Last night of all, 35
When yond same star that's westward from
    the pole
Had made his course to illume that part of heaven
Where now it burns, Marcellus and myself,
The bell then beating one,—

*(Enter GHOST.)*

*MAR.* Peace, break thee off; look, where it comes
    again! 40
*BER.* In the same figure, like the king that's dead.
*MAR.* Thou art a scholar; speak to it, Horatio.
*BER.* Looks it not like the king? mark it, Horatio.
*HOR.* Most like: it harrows me with fear and
    wonder.

*Ber.* It would be spoke to.

*Mar.* Question it, Horatio. 45

*Hor.* What art thou, that usurp'st this time of
     night,
Together with that fair and warlike form
In which the majesty of buried Denmark
Did sometimes march? by heaven I charge thee,
     speak!

*Mar.* It is offended.

*Ber.* See, it stalks away! 50

*Hor.* Stay! speak, speak! I charge thee, speak!

(*Exit* Ghost.)

*Mar.* 'Tis gone, and will not answer.

*Ber.* How now, Horatio! you tremble and look
     pale:
Is not this something more than fantasy?
What think you on't? 55

*Hor.* Before my God, I might not this believe
Without the sensible and true avouch
Of mine own eyes.

*Mar.* Is it not like the king?

*Hor.* As thou art to thyself:
Such was the very armour he had on 60
When he the ambitious Norway combated;
So frown'd he once, when, in an angry parle,
He smote the sledded Polacks on the ice.
'Tis strange.

*Mar.* Thus twice before, and jump at this dead
     hour, 65
With martial stalk hath he gone by our watch.

*Hor.* In what particular thought to work I
     know not;
But, in the gross and scope of my opinion,
This bodes some strange eruption to our state.

*Mar.* Good now, sit down, and tell me, he that
     knows, 70
Why this same strict and most observant watch
So nightly toils the subject of the land,
And why such daily cast of brazen cannon,
And foreign mart for implements of war;

Why such impress of shipwrights, whose sore
    task 75
Does not divide the Sunday from the week;
What might be toward, that this sweaty haste
Doth make the night joint-labourer with the day:
Who is't that can inform me?
*Hor.* That can I;
At least the whisper goes so. Our last king, 80
Whose image even but now appear'd to us,
Was, as you know, by Fortinbras of Norway,
Thereto prick'd on by a most emulate pride,
Dared to the combat; in which our valiant
    Hamlet—
For so this side of our known world esteem'd
    him— 85
Did slay this Fortinbras; who by a seal'd compact,
Well ratified by law and heraldry,
Did forfeit, with his life, all those his lands
Which he stood seized of, to the conqueror:
Against the which, a moiety competent 90
Was gaged by our king; which had return'd
To the inheritance of Fortinbras,
Had he been vanquisher; as, by the same covenant
And carriage of the article design'd,
His fell to Hamlet. Now, sir, young Fortinbras, 95
Of unimproved mettle hot and full,
Hath in the skirts of Norway here and there
Shark'd up a list of lawless resolutes,
For food and diet, to some enterprise
That hath a stomach in't: which is no other— 100
As it doth well appear unto our state—
But to recover of us, by strong hand
And terms compulsatory, those foresaid lands
So by his father lost: and this, I take it,
Is the main motive of our preparations, 105
The source of this our watch and the chief head
Of this post-haste and romage in the land.
*Ber.* I think it be no other but e'en so:
Well may it sort, that this portentous figure
Comes armed through our watch, so like the
    king 110
That was and is the question of these wars.

*HOR.* A mote it is to trouble the mind's eye.
In the most high and palmy state of Rome,
A little ere the mightiest Julius fell,
The graves stood tenantless, and the sheeted
    dead 115
Did squeak and gibber in the Roman streets:
. . . . . . .
As stars with trains of fire and dews of blood,
Disasters in the sun; and the moist star,
Upon whose influence Neptune's empire stands,
Was sick almost to doomsday with eclipse: 120
And even the like precurse of fierce events,
As harbingers preceding still the fates
And prologue to the omen coming on,
Have heaven and earth together demonstrated
Unto our climatures and countrymen. 125

*(Re-enter GHOST.)*

But soft, behold! lo, where it comes again!
I'll cross it, though it blast me. Stay, illusion!
If thou hast any sound, or use of voice,
Speak to me:
If there be any good thing to be done, 130
That may to thee do ease and grace to me,
Speak to me:
If thou art privy to thy country's fate,
Which, happily, foreknowing may avoid,
O, speak! 135
Or if thou hast uphoarded in thy life
Extorted treasure in the womb of earth,
For which, they say, you spirits oft walk in death,
Speak of it: stay, and speak! *(The cock crows.)* Stop it,
    Marcellus.
*MAR.* Shall I strike at it with my partisan? 140
*HOR.* Do, if it will not stand.
*BER.* 'Tis here!
*HOR.* 'Tis here!
*MAR.* 'Tis gone! *(Exit GHOST.)*
We do it wrong, being so majestical,
To offer it the show of violence;
For it is, as the air, invulnerable, 145

And our vain blows malicious mockery.
*Ber.* It was about to speak, when the cock crew.
*Hor.* And then it started like a guilty thing
Upon a fearful summons. I have heard,
The cock, that is the trumpet to the morn, 150
Doth with his lofty and shrill-sounding throat
Awake the god of day, and at his warning,
Whether in sea or fire, in earth or air,
The extravagant and erring spirit hies
To his confine: and of the truth herein 155
This present object made probation.
*Mar.* It faded on the crowing of the cock.
Some say that ever 'gainst that season comes
Wherein our Saviour's birth is celebrated,
The bird of dawning singeth all night long: 160
And then, they say, no spirit dare stir abroad,
The nights are wholesome, then no planets strike,
No fairy takes nor witch hath power to charm,
So hallow'd and so gracious is the time.
*Hor.* So have I heard and do in part believe it. 165
But look, the morn, in russet mantle clad,
Walks o'er the dew of yon high eastward hill:
Break we our watch up; and by my advice,
Let us impart what we have seen to-night
Unto young Hamlet; for, upon my life, 170
This spirit, dumb to us, will speak to him:
Do you consent we shall acquaint him with it,
As needful in our loves, fitting our duty?
*Mar.* Let's do't, I pray; and I this morning know
Where we shall find him most conveniently. *(Exeunt.)* 175

SCENE II. A ROOM OF STATE IN THE CASTLE.

*(Flourish. Enter the King, Queen, Hamlet, Polonius, Laertes, Voltimand, Cornelius, Lords, and Attendants.)*

*King.* Though yet of Hamlet our dear brother's death
The memory be green, and that it us befitted
To bear our hearts in grief and our whole kingdom

To be contracted in one brow of woe,
Yet so far hath discretion fought with nature 5
That we with wisest sorrow think on him,
Together with remembrance of ourselves.
Therefore our sometime sister, now our queen,
The imperial jointress to this warlike state,
Have we, as 'twere with a defeated joy,— 10
With an auspicious and a dropping eye,
With mirth in funeral and with dirge in marriage,
In equal scale weighing delight and dole,—
Taken to wife: nor have we herein barr'd
Your better wisdoms, which have freely gone 15
With this affair along. For all, our thanks.
Now follows, that you know, young Fortinbras,
Holding a weak supposal of our worth,
Or thinking by our late dear brother's death
Our state to be disjoint and out of frame, 20
Colleagued with this dream of his advantage,
He hath not fail'd to pester us with message,
Importing the surrender of those lands
Lost by his father, with all bonds of law,
To our most valiant brother. So much for him. 25
Now for ourself, and for this time of meeting:
Thus much the business is: we have here writ
To Norway, uncle of young Fortinbras,—
Who, impotent and bed-rid, scarcely hears
Of this his nephew's purpose,—to suppress 30
His further gait herein; in that the levies,
The lists and full proportions, are all made
Out of his subject: and we here dispatch
You, good Cornelius, and you, Voltimand,
For bearers of this greeting to old Norway, 35
Giving to you no further personal power
To business with the king more than the scope
Of these delated articles allow.
Farewell, and let your haste commend your duty.
*Cor.* } In that and all things will we show our
    duty. 40
*Vol.* }
KING. We doubt it nothing: heartily farewell.

*(Exeunt Voltimand and Cornelius.)*

And now, Laertes, what's the news with you?
You told us of some suit; what is't, Laertes?
You cannot speak of reason to the Dane,
And lose your voice: what wouldst thou beg,
 Laertes, 45
That shall not be my offer, not thy asking?
The head is not more native to the heart,
The hand more instrumental to the mouth,
Than is the throne of Denmark to thy father.
What wouldst thou have, Laertes?
*LAER.* My dread lord, 50
Your leave and favour to return to France,
From whence though willingly I came to Denmark,
To show my duty in your coronation,
Yet now, I must confess, that duty done,
My thoughts and wishes bend again toward
 France 55
And bow them to your gracious leave and pardon.
*KING.* Have you your father's leave? What says
 Polonius?
*POL.* He hath, my lord, wrung from me my slow
 leave
By laboursome petition, and at last
Upon his will I seal'd my hard consent: 60
I do beseech you, give him leave to go.
*KING.* Take thy fair hour, Laertes; time be thine,
And thy best graces spend it at thy will!
But now, my cousin Hamlet, and my son,—
*HAM.* *(Aside)* A little more than kin, and less than
 kind. 65
*KING.* How is it that the clouds still hang on you?
*HAM.* Not so, my lord; I am too much i' the sun.
*QUEEN.* Good Hamlet, cast thy nighted colour off,
And let thine eye look like a friend on Denmark.
Do not for ever with thy vailed lids 70
Seek for thy noble father in the dust:
Thou know'st 'tis common; all that lives must die,
Passing through nature to eternity.
*HAM.* Ay, madam, it is common.
*QUEEN.* If it be,
Why seems it so particular with thee? 75
*HAM.* Seems, madam! nay, it is; I know not 'seems.'

'Tis not alone my inky cloak, good mother,
Nor customary suits of solemn black,
Nor windy suspiration of forced breath,
No, nor the fruitful river in the eye, 80
Nor the dejected haviour of the visage,
Together with all forms, moods, shapes of grief,
That can denote me truly: these indeed seem,
For they are actions that a man might play:
But I have that within which passes show; 85
These but the trappings and the suits of woe.
*KING.* 'Tis sweet and commendable in your nature,
    Hamlet,
To give these mourning duties to your father:
But, you must know, your father lost a father,
That father lost, lost his, and the survivor bound 90
In filial obligation for some term
To do obsequious sorrow: but to persever
In obstinate condolement is a course
Of impious stubbornness; 'tis unmanly grief:
It shows a will most incorrect to heaven, 95
A heart unfortified, a mind impatient,
An understanding simple and unschool'd:
For what we know must be and is as common
As any the most vulgar thing to sense,
Why should we in our peevish opposition 100
Take it to heart? Fie! 'tis a fault to heaven,
A fault against the dead, a fault to nature,
To reason most absurd, whose common theme
Is death of fathers, and who still hath cried,
From the first corse till he that died to-day, 105
'This must be so.' We pray you, throw to earth
This unprevailing woe, and think of us
As of a father: for let the world take note,
You are the most immediate to our throne,
And with no less nobility of love 110
Than that which dearest father bears his son
Do I impart toward you. For your intent
In going back to school in Wittenberg,
It is most retrograde to our desire:
And we beseech you, bend you to remain 115
Here in the cheer and comfort of our eye,
Our chiefest courtier, cousin and our son.

*QUEEN.* Let not thy mother lose her prayers,
 Hamlet:
~~I pray thee, stay with us~~; go not to Wittenberg.
*HAM.* I shall in all my best obey you, madam. 120
*KING.* Why, 'tis a loving and a fair reply:
Be as ourself in Denmark. Madam, come;
This gentle and unforced accord of Hamlet
Sits smiling to my heart: in grace whereof,
No jocund health that Denmark drinks to-day, 125
But the great cannon to the clouds shall tell,
And the king's rouse the heaven shall bruit again,
Re-speaking earthly thunder. Come away.

   *(Flourish. Exeunt all but Hamlet.)*

*HAM.* O, that this too solid flesh would melt,
Thaw and resolve itself into a dew! 130
Or that the Everlasting had not fix'd
His canon 'gainst self-slaughter! O God! God!
How weary, stale, flat and unprofitable
Seem to me all the uses of this world!
Fie on't! ah fie! 'tis an unweeded garden, 135
That grows to seed; things rank and gross in nature
Possess it merely. That it should come to this!
But two months dead! nay, not so much, not two:
So excellent a king; that was, to this,
Hyperion to a satyr: so loving to my mother, 140
That he might not beteem the winds of heaven
Visit her face too roughly. Heaven and earth!
Must I remember? why, she would hang on him,
As if increase of appetite had grown
By what it fed on: and yet, within a month— 145
Let me not think on't—Frailty, thy name is woman!
 —

A little month, or ere those shoes were old
With which she follow'd my poor father's body,
Like Niobe, all tears:—why she, even she,—
O God! a beast, that wants discourse of reason, 150
Would have mourn'd longer,—married with my
 uncle,
My father's brother, but no more like my father
Than I to Hercules: within a month;

Ere yet the salt of most unrighteous tears
Had left the flushing in her galled eyes, 155
She married. O, most wicked speed, to post
With such dexterity to incestuous sheets!
It is not, nor it cannot come to good:
But break, my heart, for I must hold my tongue!

*(ENTER HORATIO, MARCELLUS, AND BERNARDO.)*

*HOR.* Hail to your lordship!
*HAM.* I am glad to see you well: 160
Horatio,—or I do forget myself.
*HOR.* The same, my lord, and your poor servant
    ever.
*HAM.* Sir, my good friend; I'll change that name
    with you:
And what make you from Wittenberg, Horatio?
Marcellus? 165
*MAR.* My good lord?
*HAM.* I am very glad to see you. *(To BER.)* Good
    even, sir.
But what, in faith, make you from Wittenberg?
*HOR.* A truant disposition, good my lord.
*HAM.* I would not hear your enemy say so, 170
Nor shall you do my ear that violence,
To make it truster of your own report
Against yourself: I know you are no truant.
But what is your affair in Elsinore?
We'll teach you to drink deep ere you depart. 175
*HOR.* My lord, I came to see your father's funeral.
*HAM.* I prethee, do not mock me, fellow-student;
I think it was to see my mother's wedding.
*HOR.* Indeed, my lord, it follow'd hard upon.
*HAM.* Thrift, thrift, Horatio! the funeral
    baked-meats 180
Did coldly furnish forth the marriage tables.
Would I had met my dearest foe in heaven
Or ever I had seen that day, Horatio!
My father!—methinks I see my father.
*HOR.* O where, my lord?
*HAM.* In my mind's eye, Horatio. 185
*HOR.* I saw him once; he was a goodly king.

*HAM.* He was a man, take him for all in all,
I shall not look upon his like again.
*HOR.* My lord, I think I saw him yesternight.
*HAM.* Saw? Who? 190
*HOR.* My lord, the king your father.
*HAM.* The king my father!
*HOR.* Season your admiration for a while
With an attent ear, till I may deliver,
Upon the witness of these gentlemen,
This marvel to you.
*HAM.* For God's love, let me hear. 195
*HOR.* Two nights together had these gentlemen,
Marcellus and Bernardo, on their watch,
In the dead vast and middle of the night,
Been thus encounter'd. A figure like your father,
Armed at point exactly, cap-a-pe, 200
Appears before them, and with solemn march
Goes slow and stately by them: thrice he walk'd
By their oppress'd and fear-surprised eyes,
Within his truncheon's length; whilst they, distill'd
Almost to jelly with the act of fear, 205
Stand dumb, and speak not to him. This to me
In dreadful secrecy impart they did;
And I with them the third night kept the watch:
Where, as they had deliver'd, both in time,
Form of the thing, each word made true and
    good, 210
The apparition comes: I knew your father;
These hands are not more like.
*HAM.* But where was this?
*MAR.* My lord, upon the platform where we
    watch'd.
*HAM.* Did you not speak to it?
*HOR.* My lord, I did,
But answer made it none: yet once methought 215
It lifted up its head and did address
Itself to motion, like as it would speak:
But even then the morning cock crew loud,
And at the sound it shrunk in haste away
And vanish'd from our sight.
*HAM.* 'Tis very strange. 220
*HOR.* As I do live, my honour'd lord, 'tis true,

And we did think it writ down in our duty
To let you know of it.

*Ham.* Indeed, indeed, sirs, but this troubles me.
Hold you the watch to-night?

*Mar.* } We do, my lord. 225
*Ber.* }

*Ham.* Arm'd, say you?

*Mar.* } Arm'd, my lord.
*Ber.* }

*Ham.* From top to toe?

*Mar.* } My lord, from head to foot.
*Ber.* }

*Ham.* Then saw you not his face?

*Hor.* O, yes, my lord; he wore his beaver up.

*Ham.* What, look'd he frowningly? 230

*Hor.* A countenance more in sorrow than in anger.

*Ham.* Pale or red?

*Hor.* Nay, very pale.

*Ham.* And fix'd his eyes upon you?

*Hor.* Most constantly.

*Ham.* I would I had been there.

*Hor.* It would have much amazed you. 235

*Ham.* Very like, very like. Stay'd it long?

*Hor.* While one with moderate haste might tell a
    hundred.

*Mar.*} Longer, longer.
*Ber.*}

*Hor.* Not when I saw't.

*Ham.* His beard was grizzled? no?

*Hor.* It was, as I have seen it in his life, 240
A sable silver'd.

*Ham.* I will watch to-night;
Perchance 'twill walk again.

*Hor.* I warrant it will.

*Ham.* If it assume my noble father's person,
I'll speak to it, though hell itself should gape
And bid me hold my peace. I pray you all, 245
If you have hitherto conceal'd this sight,
Let it be tenable in your silence still,
And whatsoever else shall hap to-night,
Give it an understanding, but no tongue:
I will requite your loves. So fare you well: 250

Upon the platform, 'twixt eleven and twelve.
I'll visit you.
*ALL.* Our duty to your honour.
*HAM.* Your loves, as mine to you: farewell.

*(Exeunt all but Hamlet.)*

My father's spirit in arms! all is not well;
I doubt some foul play: would the night were
   come! 255
Till then sit still, my soul: foul deeds will rise,
Though all the earth o'erwhelm them, to men's
   eyes. *(Exit.)*


## SCENE III. A ROOM IN POLONIUS'S HOUSE

*(ENTER LAERTES AND OPHELIA.)*

*LAER.* My necessaries are embark'd: farewell:
And, sister, as the winds give benefit
And convoy is assistant, do not sleep,
But let me hear from you.
*OPH.* Do you doubt that?
*LAER.* For Hamlet, and the trifling of his favour, 5
Hold it a fashion, and a toy in blood,
A violet in the youth of primy nature,
Forward, not permanent, sweet, not lasting,
The perfume and suppliance of a minute;
No more.
*OPH.* No more but so?
*LAER.* Think it no more: 10
For nature crescent does not grow alone
In thews and bulk; but, as this temple waxes,
The inward service of the mind and soul
Grows wide withal. Perhaps he loves you now;
And now no soil nor cautel doth besmirch 15
The virtue of his will: but you must fear,
His greatness weigh'd, his will is not his own;
For he himself is subject to his birth:
He may not, as unvalued persons do,
Carve for himself, for on his choice depends 20
The safety and health of this whole state,

And therefore must his choice be circumscribed
Unto the voice and yielding of that body
Whereof he is the head. Then if he says he
    loves you,
It fits your wisdom so far to believe it 25
As he in his particular act and place
May give his saying deed; which is no further
Than the main voice of Denmark goes withal.
Then weigh what loss your honour may sustain,
If with too credent ear you list his songs, 30
Or lose your heart, or your chaste treasure open
To his unmaster'd importunity.
Fear it, Ophelia, fear it, my dear sister,
And keep you in the rear of your affection,
Out of the shot and danger of desire. 35
The chariest maid is prodigal enough,
If she unmask her beauty to the moon:
Virtue itself 'scapes not calumnious strokes:
The canker galls the infants of the spring
Too oft before their buttons be disclosed, 40
And in the morn and liquid dew of youth
Contagious blastments are most imminent.
Be wary then; best safety lies in fear:
Youth to itself rebels, though none else near.
OPH. I shall the effect of this good lesson keep, 45
As watchman to my heart. But, good my
    brother,
Do not, as some ungracious pastors do,
Show me the steep and thorny way to heaven,
Whilst, like a puff'd and reckless libertine,
Himself the primrose path of dalliance treads 50
And recks not his own rede.
LAER. O, fear me not.
I stay too long: but here my father comes.

*(ENTER POLONIUS.)*

A double blessing is a double grace;
Occasion smiles upon a second leave.
POL. Yet here, Laertes! Aboard, aboard, for
    shame! 55
The wind sits in the shoulder of your sail,

And you are stay'd for. There; my blessing with
    thee!
And these few precepts in thy memory
Look thou character. Give thy thoughts no
    tongue,
Nor any unproportion'd thought his act. 60
Be thou familiar, but by no means vulgar.
Those friends thou hast, and their adoption tried,
Grapple them to thy soul with hoops of steel,
But do not dull thy palm with entertainment
Of each new-hatch'd, unfledged comrade.
    Beware 65
Of entrance to a quarrel; but being in,
Bear't, that th' opposed may beware of thee.
Give every man thy ear, but few thy voice:
Take each man's censure, but reserve thy
    judgement.
Costly thy habit as thy purse can buy, 70
But not express'd in fancy; rich, not gaudy:
For the apparel oft proclaims the man;
And they in France of the best rank and station
Are of a most select and generous chief in that.
Neither a borrower nor a lender be: 75
For loan oft loses both itself and friend,
And borrowing dulls the edge of husbandry.
This above all: to thine own self be true,
And it must follow, as the night the day,
Thou canst not then be false to any man. 80
Farewell: my blessing season this in thee!
*Laer.* Most humbly do I take my leave, my lord.
*Pol.* The time invites you; go, your servants tend.
*Laer.* Farewell, Ophelia, and remember well
What I have said to you.
*Oph.* 'Tis in my memory lock'd, 85
And you yourself shall keep the key of it.
*Laer.* Farewell. *(Exit.)*
*Pol.* What is't, Ophelia, he hath said to you?
*Oph.* So please you, something touching the Lord
    Hamlet.
*Pol.* Marry, well bethought: 90
'Tis told me, he hath very oft of late
Given private time to you, and you yourself

Have of your audience been most free and
    bounteous:
If it be so—as so 'tis put on me,
And that in way of caution—I must tell you, 95
You do not understand yourself so clearly
As it behoves my daughter and your honour.
What is between you? give me up the truth.
*Oph.* He hath, my lord, of late made many tenders
Of his affection to me. 100
*Pol.* Affection! pooh! you speak like a green girl,
Unsifted in such perilous circumstance.
Do you believe his tenders, as you call them?
*Oph.* I do not know, my lord, what I should think.
*Pol.* Marry, I'll teach you: think yourself a baby, 105
That you have ta'en these tenders for true pay,
Which are not sterling. Tender yourself more
    dearly;
Or—not to crack the wind of the poor phrase,
Running it thus—you'll tender me a fool.
*Oph.* My lord, he hath importuned me with love 110
In honourable fashion.
*Pol.* Ay, fashion you may call it; go to, go to.
*Oph.* And hath given countenance to his speech,
    my lord,
With almost all the holy vows of heaven.
*Pol.* Ay, springes to catch woodcocks. I do
    know, 115
When the blood burns, how prodigal the soul
Lends the tongue vows: these blazes, daughter,
Giving more light than heat, extinct in both,
Even in their promise, as it is a-making,
You must not take for fire. From this time 120
Be something scanter of your maiden presence;
Set your entreatments at a higher rate
Than a command to parley. For Lord Hamlet,
Believe so much in him, that he is young,
And with a larger tether may he walk 125
Than may be given you: in few, Ophelia,
Do not believe his vows; for they are brokers,
Not of that dye which their investments show,
But mere implorators of unholy suits,
Breathing like sanctified and pious bawds, 130

The better to beguile. This is for all:
I would not, in plain terms, from this time forth,
Have you so slander any moment leisure,
As to give words or talk with the Lord Hamlet.
Look to't, I charge you: come your ways. 135
*Oph.* I shall obey, my lord. *(Exeunt.)*


SCENE IV. THE PLATFORM: (ENTER HAMLET,
HORATIO, AND MARCELLUS.)

*Ham.* The air bites shrewdly; it is very cold.
*Hor.* It is a nipping and an eager air.
*Ham.* What hour now?
*Hor.* I think it lacks of twelve.
*Mar.* No, it is struck.
*Hor.* Indeed? I heard it not: it then draws near the
season 5
Wherein the spirit held his wont to walk.

*(A flourish of trumpets, and ordnance shot off within.)*

What does this mean, my lord?
*Ham.* The king doth wake to-night and takes his
rouse,
Keeps wassail, and the swaggering up-spring reels;
And as he drains his draughts of Rhenish down, 10
The kettle-drum and trumpet thus bray out
The triumph of his pledge.
*Hor.* Is it a custom?
*Ham.* Ay, marry, is't:
But to my mind, though I am native here
And to the manner born, it is a custom 15
More honour'd in the breach than the observance.
This heavy-headed revel east and west
Makes us traduced and tax'd of other nations:
They clepe us drunkards, and with swinish phrase
Soil our addition; and indeed it takes 20
From our achievements, though perform'd at
height,
The pith and marrow of our attribute.
So, oft it chances in particular men,
That for some vicious mole of nature in them,

As, in their birth,—wherein they are not guilty, 25
Since nature cannot choose his origin,—
By the o'ergrowth of some complexion,
Oft breaking down the pales and forts of reason,
Or by some habit that too much o'er-leavens
The form of plausive manners, that these men,— 30
Carrying, I say, the stamp of one defect,
Being nature's livery, or fortune's star,—
Their virtues else—be they as pure as grace,
As infinite as man may undergo—
Shall in the general censure take corruption 35
From that particular fault: the dram of eale
Doth all the noble substance of a doubt
To his own scandal.

*(Enter Ghost.)*

HOR. Look, my lord, it comes!
HAM. Angels and ministers of grace defend us!
Be thou a spirit of health or goblin damn'd, 40
Bring with thee airs from heaven or blasts from
    hell,
Be thy intents wicked or charitable,
Thou comest in such a questionable shape
That I will speak to thee: I'll call thee Hamlet,
King, father, royal Dane: O, answer me! 45
Let me not burst in ignorance; but tell
Why thy canonized bones, hearsed in death,
Have burst their cerements; why the sepulchre,
Wherein we saw thee quietly inurn'd,
Hath oped his ponderous and marble jaws, 50
To cast thee up again. What may this mean,
That thou, dead corse, again, in complete steel,
Revisit'st thus the glimpses of the moon,
Making night hideous; and we fools of nature
So horridly to shake our disposition 55
With thoughts beyond the reaches of our souls?
Say, why is this? wherefore? what should we do?

*(Ghost beckons Hamlet.)*

HOR. It beckons you to go away with it,

As if it some impartment did desire
To you alone.
*Mar.* Look, with what courteous action 60
It waves you to a more removed ground:
But do not go with it.
*Hor.* No, by no means.
*Ham.* It will not speak; then I will follow it.
*Hor.* Do not, my lord.
*Ham.* Why, what should be the fear?
I do not set my life at a pin's fee; 65
And for my soul, what can it do to that,
Being a thing immortal as itself?
It waves me forth again: I'll follow it.
*Hor.* What if it tempt you toward the flood, my
    lord,
Or to the dreadful summit of the cliff 70
That beetles o'er his base into the sea,
And there assume some other horrible form,
Which might deprive your sovereignty of reason
And draw you into madness? think of it:
The very place puts toys of desperation, 75
Without more motive, into every brain
That looks so many fathoms to the sea
And hears it roar beneath.
*Ham.* It waves me still.
Go on; I'll follow thee.
*Mar.* You shall not go, my lord.
*Ham.* Hold off your hands. 80
*Hor.* Be ruled; you shall not go.
*Ham.* My fate cries out,
And makes each petty artery in this body
As hardy as the Nemean lion's nerve.
Still am I call'd: unhand me, gentlemen;
By heaven, I'll make a ghost of him that lets
    me: 85
I say, away! Go on; I'll follow thee.

*(Exeunt Ghost and Hamlet.)*

*Hor.* He waxes desperate with imagination.
*Mar.* Let's follow; 'tis not fit thus to obey him.
*Hor.* Have after. To what issue will this come?

*MAR.* Something is rotten in the state of
  Denmark. 90
*HOR.* Heaven will direct it.
*MAR.* Nay, let's follow him. *(Exeunt.)*


SCENE V. ANOTHER PART OF THE PLATFORM:
(ENTER GHOST AND HAMLET.)

*HAM.* Whither wilt thou lead me? speak; I'll go no
  further.
*GHOST.* Mark me.
*HAM.* I will.
*GHOST.* My hour is almost come,
When I to sulphurous and tormenting flames
Must render up myself.
*HAM.* Alas, poor ghost!
*GHOST.* Pity me not, but lend thy serious hearing 5
To what I shall unfold.
*HAM.* Speak; I am bound to hear.
*GHOST.* So art thou to revenge, when thou shalt
  hear.
*HAM.* What?
*GHOST.* I am thy father's spirit;
Doom'd for a certain term to walk the night, 10
And for the day confined to fast in fires,
Till the foul crimes done in my days of nature
Are burnt and purged away. But that I am forbid
To tell the secrets of my prison-house,
I could a tale unfold whose lightest word 15
Would harrow up thy soul, freeze thy young blood,
Make thy two eyes, like stars, start from their
  spheres,
Thy knotted and combined locks to part
And each particular hair to stand an end,
Like quills upon the fretful porpentine: 20
But this eternal blazon must not be
To ears of flesh and blood. List, list, O, list!
If thou didst ever thy dear father love—
*HAM.* O God!
*GHOST.* Revenge his foul and most unnatural
  murder. 25
*HAM.* Murder!

*GHOST.* Murder most foul, as in the best it is,
But this most foul, strange, and unnatural.
*HAM.* Haste me to know't, that I, with wings as
    swift
As meditation or the thoughts of love, 30
May sweep to my revenge.
*GHOST.* I find thee apt;
And duller shouldst thou be than the fat weed
That roots itself in ease on Lethe wharf,
Wouldst thou not stir in this. Now, Hamlet, hear:
'Tis given out that, sleeping in my orchard, 35
A serpent stung me; so the whole ear of Denmark
Is by a forged process of my death
Rankly abused: but know, thou noble youth,
The serpent that did sting thy father's life
Now wears his crown.
*HAM.* O my prophetic soul! 40
My uncle!
*GHOST.* Ay, that incestuous, that adulterate beast,
With witchcraft of his wit, with traitorous gifts,—
O wicked wit and gifts, that have the power
So to seduce!—won to his shameful lust 45
The will of my most seeming-virtuous queen:
O Hamlet, what a falling-off was there!
From me, whose love was of that dignity
That it went hand in hand even with the vow
I made to her in marriage; and to decline 50
Upon a wretch, whose natural gifts were poor
To those of mine!
But virtue, as it never will be moved,
Though lewdness court it in a shape of heaven,
So lust, though to a radiant angel link'd, 55
Will sate itself in a celestial bed
And prey on garbage.
But, soft! methinks I scent the morning air;
Brief let me be. Sleeping within my orchard,
My custom always of the afternoon, 60
Upon my secure hour thy uncle stole,
With juice of cursed hebenon in a vial,
And in the porches of my ears did pour
The leperous distilment; whose effect
Holds such an enmity with blood of man 65

That swift as quicksilver it courses through
The natural gates and alleys of the body;
And with a sudden vigour it doth posset
And curd, like eager droppings into milk,
The thin and wholesome blood: so did it mine; 70
And a most instant tetter bark'd about,
Most lazar-like, with vile and loathsome crust,
All my smooth body.
Thus was I, sleeping, by a brother's hand
Of life, of crown, of queen, at once dispatch'd: 75
Cut off even in the blossoms of my sin,
Unhousel'd, disappointed, unanel'd;
No reckoning made, but sent to my account
With all my imperfections on my head:
O, horrible! O, horrible! most horrible! 80
If thou hast nature in thee, bear it not;
Let not the royal bed of Denmark be
A couch for luxury and damned incest.
But, howsoever thou pursuest this act,
Taint not thy mind, nor let thy soul contrive 85
Against thy mother aught: leave her to heaven,
And to those thorns that in her bosom lodge,
To prick and sting her. Fare thee well at once!
The glow-worm shows the matin to be near,
And 'gins to pale his uneffectual fire: 90
Adieu, adieu, adieu! remember me. *(Exit.)*
*Ham.* O all you host of heaven! O earth! what else?
And shall I couple hell? O, fie! Hold, hold, my
  heart;
And you, my sinews, grow not instant old,
But bear me stiffly up. Remember thee! 95
Ay, thou poor ghost, while memory holds a seat
In this distracted globe. Remember thee!
Yea, from the table of my memory
I'll wipe away all trivial fond records,
All saws of books, all forms, all pressures past, 100
That youth and observation copied there;
And thy commandment all alone shall live
Within the book and volume of my brain,
Unmix'd with baser matter: yes, by heaven!
O most pernicious woman! 105
0 villain, villain, smiling, damned villain!

My tables,—meet it is I set it down,
That one may smile, and smile, and be a villain;
At least I'm sure it may be so in Denmark.
*(Writing.)*
So, uncle, there you are. Now to my word; 110
It is 'Adieu, adieu! remember me.'
I have sworn't.
HOR.} *(Within)* My lord, my lord!
MAR.}

*(ENTER HORATIO AND MARCELLUS.)*

MAR. Lord Hamlet!
HOR. Heaven secure him!
HAM. So be it!
MAR. Illo, ho, ho, my lord! 115
HAM. Hillo, ho, ho, boy! come, bird, come.
MAR. How is't, my noble lord?
HOR. What news, my lord?
HAM. O, wonderful!
HOR. Good my lord, tell it.
HAM. No; you will reveal it.
HOR. Not I, my lord, by heaven.
MAR. Nor I, my lord. 120
HAM. How say you, then; would heart of man once
    think it?
But you'll be secret?
HOR.} Ay, by heaven, my lord.
MAR.}
HAM. There's ne'er a villain dwelling in all
    Denmark
But he's an arrant knave.
HOR. There needs no ghost, my lord, come from
    the grave 125
To tell us this.
HAM. Why, right; you are i' the right;
And so, without more circumstance at all,
I hold it fit that we shake hands and part:
You, as your business and desire shall point you;
For every man hath business and desire, 130
Such as it is; and for my own poor part,
Look you, I'll go pray.

*Hor.* These are but wild and whirling words, my
    lord.

*Ham.* I'm sorry they offend you, heartily;
Yes, faith, heartily.

*Hor.* There's no offence, my lord. 135

*Ham.* Yes, by Saint Patrick, but there is, Horatio,
And much offence too. Touching this vision here,
It is an honest ghost, that let me tell you:
For your desire to know what is between us,
O'ermaster't as you may. And now, good friends,

140
As you are friends, scholars and soldiers,
Give me one poor request.

*Hor.* What is't, my lord? we will.

*Ham.* Never make known what you have seen to-
    night.

*Hor.}*

*Mar.}* My lord, we will not.

*Ham.* Nay, but swear't.

*Hor.* In faith, 145
My lord, not I.

*Mar.* Nor I, my lord, in faith.

*Ham.* Upon my sword.

*Mar.* We have sworn, my lord, already.

*Ham.* Indeed, upon my sword, indeed.

*Ghost. (Beneath) Swear.*

*Ham.* Ah, ha, boy! say'st thou so? art thou there,
    true-penny? 150
Come on: you hear this fellow in the cellarage:
Consent to swear.

*Hor.* Propose the oath, my lord.

*Ham.* Never to speak of this that you have seen,
Swear by my sword.

*Ghost. (Beneath) Swear.* 155

*Ham.* Hic et ubique? then we'll shift our ground.
Come hither, gentlemen,
And lay your hands again upon my sword:
Never to speak of this that you have heard,
Swear by my sword. 160

*Ghost. (Beneath) Swear.*

*Ham.* Well said, old mole! canst work i' the earth so
    fast?

A worthy pioner! Once more remove, good friends.
*Hor.* O day and night, but this is wondrous
    strange!
*Ham.* And therefore as a stranger give it welcome.

165
There are more things in heaven and earth,
    Horatio,
Than are dreamt of in your philosophy.
But come;
Here, as before, never, so help you mercy,
How strange or odd soe'er I bear myself, 170
As I perchance hereafter shall think meet
To put an antic disposition on,
That you, at such times seeing me, never shall,
With arms encumber'd thus, or this head-shake,
Or by pronouncing of some doubtful phrase, 175
As 'Well, well, we know,' or 'We could, an if we
    would,'
Or 'If we list to speak,' or 'There be, an if they
    might,'
Or such ambiguous giving out, to note
That you know aught of me: this not to do,
So grace and mercy at your most need help you, 180
Swear.
*Ghost.* *(Beneath)* Swear.
*Ham.* Rest, rest, perturbed spirit! *(They swear.)* So,
    gentlemen,
With all my love I do commend me to you:
And what so poor a man as Hamlet is 185
May do, to express his love and friending to you,
God willing, shall not lack. Let us go in together;
And still your fingers on your lips, I pray.
The time is out of joint: O cursed spite,
That ever I was born to set it right! 190
Nay, come, let's go together. *(Exeunt.)*

# ACT II

## SCENE I. A ROOM IN POLONIUS'S HOUSE.

*(ENTER POLONIUS AND REYNALDO.)*

POL. Give him this money and these notes,
    Reynaldo.
REY. I will, my lord.
POL. You shall do marvellous wisely, good
    Reynaldo,
Before you visit him, to make inquire
Of his behaviour.
REY. My lord, I did intend it. 5
POL. Marry, well said, very well said. Look you, sir,
Inquire me first what Danskers are in Paris,
And how, and who, what means, and where they
    keep,
What company, at what expense, and finding
By this encompassment and drift of question 10
That they do know my son, come you more nearer
Than your particular demands will touch it:
Take you, as 'twere, some distant knowledge
    of him,
As thus, 'I know his father and his friends,
And in part him:' do you mark this, Reynaldo? 15
REY. Ay, very well, my lord.
POL. 'And in part him; but,' you may say, 'not well:
But if't be he I mean, he's very wild,

Addicted so and so;' and there put on him
What forgeries you please; marry, none so rank 20
As may dishonour him; take heed of that;
But, sir, such wanton, wild and usual slips
As are companions noted and most known
To youth and liberty.
REY. As gaming, my lord.
POL. Ay, or drinking, fencing, swearing, quar-
    relling, 25
Drabbing: you may go so far.
REY. My lord, that would dishonour him.
POL. Faith, no; as you may season it in the charge.
You must not put another scandal on him,
That he is open to incontinency; 30
That's not my meaning: but breathe his faults so
    quaintly
That they may seem the taints of liberty,
The flash and outbreak of a fiery mind,
A savageness in unreclaimed blood,
Of general assault.
REY. But, my good lord,— 35
POL. Wherefore should you do this?
REY. Ay, my lord,
I would know that.
POL. Marry, sir, here's my drift,
And I believe it is a fetch of warrant:
You laying these slight sullies on my son,
As 'twere a thing a little soil'd i' the working, 40
Mark you,
Your party in converse, him you would sound,
Having ever seen in the prenominate crimes
The youth you breathe of guilty, be assured
He closes with you in this consequence; 45
'Good sir,' or so, or 'friend,' or 'gentleman,'
According to the phrase or the addition
Of man and country.
REY. Very good, my lord.
POL. And then, sir, does he this—he does—what
    was I
about to say? By the mass, I was about to say some-
    thing: 50
where did I leave?

REY. At 'closes in the consequence,' at 'friend
    or so,'
and 'gentleman.'
POL. At 'closes in the consequence,' ay, marry;
He closes with you thus: 'I know the gentleman; 55
I saw him yesterday, or t'other day,
Or then, or then, with such, or such, and, as
    you say,
There was a' gaming, there o'ertook in's rouse,
There falling out at tennis:' or perchance,
'I saw him enter such a house of sale,' 60
Videlicet, a brothel, or so forth.
See you now;
Your bait of falsehood takes this carp of truth:
And thus do we of wisdom and of reach,
With windlasses and with assays of bias, 65
By indirections find directions out:
So, by my former lecture and advice,
Shall you my son. You have me, have you not?
REY. My lord, I have.
POL. God be wi' ye; fare ye well.
REY. Good my lord! 70
POL. Observe his inclination in yourself.
REY. I shall, my lord.
POL. And let him ply his music.
REY. Well, my lord.
POL. Farewell! *(Exit Reynaldo.)*

*(ENTER OPHELIA.)*

How now, Ophelia! what's the matter?
OPH. O, my lord, my lord, I have been so af-
    frighted! 75
POL. With what, i' the name of God?
OPH. My lord, as I was sewing in my closet,
Lord Hamlet, with his doublet all unbraced,
No hat upon his head, his stockings foul'd,
Ungarter'd and down-gyved to his ancle; 80
Pale as his shirt, his knees knocking each other,
And with a look so piteous in purport
As if he had been loosed out of hell
To speak of horrors, he comes before me.

*Pol.* Mad for thy love?
*Oph.* My lord, I do not know, 85
But truly I do fear it.
*Pol.* What said he?
*Oph.* He took me by the wrist and held me hard;
Then goes he to the length of all his arm,
And with his other hand thus o'er his brow,
He falls to such perusal of my face 90
As he would draw it. Long stay'd he so;
At last, a little shaking of mine arm,
And thrice his head thus waving up and down,
He raised a sigh so piteous and profound
As it did seem to shatter all his bulk 95
And end his being: that done, he lets me go:
And with his head over his shoulder turn'd,
He seem'd to find his way without his eyes;
For out o' doors he went without their helps,
And to the last bended their light on me. 100
*Pol.* Come, go with me: I will go seek the king.
This is the very ecstasy of love;
Whose violent property fordoes itself
And leads the will to desperate undertakings
As oft as any passion under heaven 105
That does afflict our natures. I am sorry.
What, have you given him any hard words of late?
*Oph.* No, my good lord, but, as you did command,
I did repel his letters and denied
His access to me.
*Pol.* That hath made him mad. 110
I am sorry that with better heed and judgement
I had not quoted him: I fear'd he did but trifle
And meant to wreck thee; but beshrew my
      jealousy!
By heaven, it is as proper to our age
To cast beyond ourselves in our opinions 115
As it is common for the younger sort
To lack discretion. Come, go we to the king:
This must be known; which, being kept close,
      might move
More grief to hide than hate to utter love.
Come. *(Exeunt.)* 120

## SCENE II. A ROOM IN THE CASTLE

*(Flourish. Enter King, Queen, Rosencrantz, Guildenstern, and Attendants.)*

KING. Welcome, dear Rosencrantz and
    Guildenstern!
Moreover that we much did long to see you,
The need we have to use you did provoke
Our hasty sending. Something have you heard
Of Hamlet's transformation; so call it, 5
Sith nor the exterior nor the inward man
Resembles that it was. What it should be,
More than his father's death, that thus hath
    put him
So much from th' understanding of himself,
I cannot dream of: I entreat you both, 10
That, being of so young days brought up with him
And sith so neighbour'd to his youth and haviour,
That you vouchsafe your rest here in our court
Some little time: so by your companies
To draw him on to pleasures, and to gather 15
So much as from occasion you may glean,
Whether aught to us unknown afflicts him thus,
That open'd lies within our remedy.
QUEEN. Good gentlemen, he hath much talk'd
    of you,
And sure I am two men there are not living 20
To whom he more adheres. If it will please you
To show us so much gentry and good will
As to expend your time with us awhile
For the supply and profit of our hope,
Your visitation shall receive such thanks 25
As fits a king's remembrance.
Ros. Both your majesties
Might, by the sovereign power you have of us,
Put your dread pleasures more into command
Than to entreat.
GUIL. But we both obey,
And here give up ourselves, in the full bent 30
To lay our service freely at your feet,
To be commanded.

*King.* Thanks, Rosencrantz and gentle
    Guildenstern.
*Queen.* Thanks, Guildenstern and gentle
    Rosencrantz:
And I beseech you instantly to visit 35
My too much changed son. Go, some of you,
And bring these gentlemen where Hamlet is.
*Guil.* Heavens make our presence and our
    practices
Pleasant and helpful to him!
*Queen.* Ay, amen!

*(Exeunt Rosencrantz, Guildenstern, and some Attendants.)*

*(ENTER POLONIUS.)*

*Pol.* The ambassadors from Norway, my good
    lord, 40
Are joyfully return'd.
*King.* Thou still hast been the father of good news.
*Pol.* Have I, my lord? I assure my good liege,
I hold my duty as I hold my soul,
Both to my God and to my gracious king: 45
And I do think, or else this brain of mine
Hunts not the trail of policy so sure
As it hath used to do, that I have found
The very cause of Hamlet's lunacy.
*King.* O, speak of that; that do I long to hear. 50
*Pol.* Give first admittance to the ambassadors;
My news shall be the fruit to that great feast.
*King.* Thyself do grace to them, and bring them in.

*(Exit Polonius.)*

He tells me, my dear Gertrude, he hath found
The head and source of all your son's distemper. 55
*Queen.* I doubt it is no other but the main;
His father's death and our o'erhasty marriage.
*King.* Well, we shall sift him.

*(RE-ENTER POLONIUS, WITH VOLTIMAND AND CORNELIUS.)*

Welcome, my good friends!
Say, Voltimand, what from our brother Norway?
*Volt.* Most fair return of greetings and desires. ₆₀
Upon our first, he sent out to suppress
His nephew's levies, which to him appear'd
To be a preparation 'gainst the Polack,
But better look'd into, he truly found
It was against your highness: whereat grieved, ₆₅
That so his sickness, age and impotence
Was falsely borne in hand, sends out arrests
On Fortinbras; which he, in brief, obeys,
Receives rebuke from Norway, and in fine
Makes vow before his uncle never more ₇₀
To give the assay of arms against your majesty.
Whereon old Norway, overcome with joy,
Gives him three thousand crowns in annual fee
And his commission to employ those soldiers,
So levied as before, against the Polack: ₇₅
With an entreaty, herein further shown, *(Giving a
    paper.)*
That it might please you to give quiet pass
Through your dominions for this enterprise,
On such regards of safety and allowance
As therein are set down.
*King.* It likes us well, ₈₀
And at our more consider'd time we'll read,
Answer, and think upon this business.
Meantime we thank you for your well-took labour:
Go to your rest; at night we'll feast together:
*Most welcome home! (Exeunt Voltimand and
    Cornelius.)*
*Pol.* This business is well ended. ₈₅
My liege, and madam, to expostulate
What majesty should be, what duty is,
Why day is day, night, and time is time,
Were nothing but to waste night, day and time.
Therefore, since brevity is the soul of wit ₉₀
And tediousness the limbs and outward flourishes,
I will be brief. Your noble son is mad:
Mad call I it; for, to define true madness,
What is't but to be nothing else but mad?
But let that go.

*QUEEN.* More matter, with less art. 95
*POL.* Madam, I swear I use no art at all.
That he is mad, 'tis true: 'tis true 'tis pity,
And pity 'tis 'tis true: a foolish figure;
But farewell it, for I will use no art.
Mad let us grant him then: and now remains 100
That we find out the cause of this effect,
Or rather say, the cause of this defect,
For this effect defective comes by cause:
Thus it remains and the remainder thus.
Perpend. 105
I have a daughter,—have while she is mine,—
Who in her duty and obedience, mark,
Hath given me this: now gather and surmise.
    *(Reads.)*
'To the celestial, and my soul's idol, the most beau-
    tified Ophelia,'—
That's an ill phrase, a vile phrase; 'beautified' is a
    vile 110
phrase: but you shall hear. Thus: *(Reads.)*
'In her excellent white bosom, these,' &c.
*QUEEN.* Came this from Hamlet to her?
*POL.* Good madam, stay awhile; I will be faithful.
    *(Reads.)*
'Doubt thou the stars are fire; 115
Doubt that the sun doth move;
Doubt truth to be a liar;
But never doubt I love.
'O dear Ophelia, I am ill at these numbers; I
    have not
art to reckon my groans: but that I love thee best, O
    most 120
best, believe it. Adieu.
'Thine evermore, most dear lady, whilst this
machine is to him, Hamlet.'
This in obedience hath my daughter shown me;
And more above, hath his solicitings, 125
As they fell out by time, by means and place,
All given to mine ear.
*KING.* But how hath she
Received his love?
*POL.* What do you think of me?

*KING.* As of a man faithful and honourable.

*POL.* I would fain prove so. But what might you
   think, 130
When I had seen this hot love on the wing,—
As I perceived it, I must tell you that,
Before my daughter told me,—what might you,
Or my dear majesty your queen here, think,
If I had play'd the desk or table-book, 135
Or given my heart a winking, mute and dumb,
Or look'd upon this love with idle sight;
What might you think? No, I went round to work,
And my young mistress thus I did bespeak:
'Lord Hamlet is a prince, out of thy star; 140
This must not be:' and then I prescripts gave her,
That she should lock herself from his resort,
Admit no messengers, receive no tokens.
Which done, she took the fruits of my advice;
And he repulsed, a short tale to make, 145
Fell into a sadness, then into a fast,
Thence to a watch, thence into a weakness,
Thence to a lightness, and by this declension
Into the madness wherein now he raves
And all we mourn for. 150

*KING.* Do you think this?

*QUEEN.* It may be, very like.

*POL.* Hath there been such a time, I'ld fain know
   that,
That I have positively said ''tis so,'
When it proved otherwise?

*KING.* Not that I know.

*POL.* (*Pointing to his head and shoulder*) Take this
   from this, if this be otherwise: 155
If circumstances lead me, I will find
Where truth is hid, though it were hid indeed
Within the centre.

*KING.* How may we try it further?

*POL.* You know, sometimes he walks four hours
   together
Here in the lobby.

*QUEEN.* So he does, indeed. 160

*POL.* At such a time I'll loose my daughter to him:
Be you and I behind an arras then;

Mark the encounter: if he love her not,
And be not from his reason fall'n thereon,
Let me be no assistant for a state, 165
But keep a farm and carters.
KING. We will try it.
QUEEN. But look where sadly the poor wretch
    comes reading.
POL. Away, I do beseech you, both away:
I'll board him presently.

*(Exeunt King, Queen, and Attendants.)*

*(Enter HAMLET, reading.)*

O, give me leave: how does my good Lord
    Hamlet? 170
HAM. Well, God-a-mercy.
POL. Do you know me, my lord?
HAM. Excellent well; you are a fishmonger.
POL. Not I, my lord.
HAM. Then I would you were so honest a man. 175
POL. Honest, my lord!
HAM. Ay, sir; to be honest, as this world goes, is to
be one man picked out of ten thousand.
POL. That's very true, my lord.
HAM. For if the sun breed maggots in a dead
    dog, 180
being a god kissing carrion—Have you a daughter?
POL. I have, my lord.
HAM. Let her not walk i' the sun: conception is a
blessing; but as your daughter may conceive,—
    friend, look
to't. 185
POL. *(Aside)* How say you by that? Still harping on
my daughter: yet he knew me not at first; he said I
    was a
fishmonger: he is far gone: and truly in my youth I
suffered much extremity for love; very near this. I'll
speak to him again. What do you read, my lord? 190
HAM. Words, words, words.
POL. What is the matter, my lord?
HAM. Between who?

*Pol.* I mean, the matter that you read, my lord.

*Ham.* Slanders, sir: for the satirical rogue says here that 195
old men have grey beards, that their faces are wrinkled,
their eyes purging thick amber and plum-tree gum, and
that they have a plentiful lack of wit, together with most
weak hams: all which, sir, though I most power-fully and
potently believe, yet I hold it not honesty to have it thus 200
set down; for yourself, sir, shall grow old as I am, if like a
crab you could go backward.

*Pol. (Aside)* Though this be madness, yet there is method in't. Will you walk out of the air, my lord?

*Ham.* Into my grave. 205

*Pol.* Indeed, that's out of the air. *(Aside)* How pregnant
sometimes his replies are! a happiness that often madness
hits on, which reason and sanity could not so pros-perously
be delivered of. I will leave him, and suddenly contrive
the means of meeting between him and my daugh-ter. My 210
honourable lord, I will most humbly take my leave of you.

*Ham.* You cannot, sir, take from me any thing that I
will more willingly part withal: except my life, ex-cept my
life, except my life.

*Pol.* Fare you well, my lord. 215

*Ham.* These tedious old fools!

*(ENTER ROSENCRANTZ AND GUILDENSTERN.)*

*Pol.* You go to seek the Lord Hamlet; there he is.

*Ros. (To Polonius) God save you, sir! (Exit Polonius.)*

*Guil.* My honoured lord!

*Ros.* My most dear lord! 220

*Ham.* My excellent good friends! How dost thou,
Guildenstern?

Ah, Rosencrantz! Good lads, how do you both?

*Ros.* As the indifferent children of the earth.

*Guil.* Happy, in that we are not over-happy;

On Fortune's cap we are not the very button. 225

*Ham.* Nor the soles of her shoe?

*Ros.* Neither, my lord.

*Ham.* Then you live about her waist, or in the
middle

of her favours?

*Guil.* Faith, her privates we. 230

*Ham.* In the secret parts of Fortune? O, most true;

she is a strumpet. What's the news?

*Ros.* None, my lord, but that the world's grown
honest.

*Ham.* Then is doomsday near: but your news is not

true. Let me question more in particular: what have
you, 235

my good friends, deserved at the hands of Fortune,
that she

sends you to prison hither?

*Guil.* Prison, my lord!

*Ham.* Denmark's a prison.

*Ros.* Then is the world one. 240

*Ham.* A goodly one; in which there are many
confines,

wards and dungeons, Denmark being one o' the
worst.

*Ros.* We think not so, my lord.

*Ham.* Why, then 'tis none to you; for there is
nothing

either good or bad, but thinking makes it so: to me
it is a 245

prison.

*Ros.* Why, then your ambition makes it one; 'tis too

narrow for your mind.

*Ham.* O God, I could be bounded in a nut-shell and

count myself a king of infinite space, were it not
that I 250

have bad dreams.

*Guil.* Which dreams indeed are ambition; for the very

substance of the ambitious is merely the shadow of a dream.

*Ham.* A dream itself is but a shadow.

*Ros.* Truly, and I hold ambition of so airy and light a $_{255}$

quality that it is but a shadow's shadow.

*Ham.* Then are our beggars bodies, and our monarchs

and outstretched heroes the beggars' shadows. Shall we to

the court? for, by my fay, I cannot reason.

*Ros. Guil.* We'll wait upon you. $_{260}$

*Ham.* No such matter: I will not sort you with the rest

of my servants; for, to speak to you like an honest man, I

am most dreadfully attended. But, in the beaten way of

friendship, what make you at Elsinore?

*Ros.* To visit you, my lord; no other occasion. $_{265}$

*Ham.* Beggar that I am, I am even poor in thanks; but

I thank you: and sure, dear friends, my thanks are too dear

a halfpenny. Were you not sent for? Is it your own

inclining? Is it a free visitation? Come, deal justly with me:

come, come; nay, speak. $_{270}$

*Guil.* What should we say, my lord?

*Ham.* Why, any thing, but to the purpose. You were

sent for; and there is a kind of confession in your looks,

which your modesties have not craft enough to colour: I

know the good king and queen have sent for you. $_{275}$

*Ros.* To what end, my lord?

*Ham.* That you must teach me. But let me conjure you,

by the rights of our fellowship, by the consonancy
  of our
youth, by the obligation of our ever-preserved love,
  and by
what more dear a better proposer could charge you
  withal, be $_{280}$
even and direct with me, whether you were sent
  for, or no.
*Ros.* *(Aside to GUIL.) What say you?*
*HAM.* *(Aside)* Nay then, I have an eye of you.
    —If you
love me, hold not off.
*GUIL.* My lord, we were sent for. $_{285}$
*HAM.* I will tell you why; so shall my anticipation
  prevent
your discovery, and your secrecy to the king and
  queen
moult no feather. I have of late—but wherefore I
  know not—lost
all my mirth, foregone all custom of exercises; and
  indeed
it goes so heavily with my disposition that this
  goodly $_{290}$
frame, the earth, seems to me a sterile promontory;
  this most
excellent canopy, the air, look you, this brave o'er-
  hanging
firmament, this majestical roof fretted with golden
  fire, why,
it appears no other thing to me than a foul and
  pestilent
congregation of vapours. What a piece of work is a
  man! $_{295}$
how noble in reason! how infinite in faculty! in
  form and
moving how express and admirable! in action how
  like an
angel! in apprehension how like a god! the beauty
  of the
world! the paragon of animals! And yet, to me,
  what is this

quintessence of dust? man delights not me; no, nor
woman 300
neither, though by your smiling you seem to say so.

*Ros.* My lord, there was no such stuff in my
thoughts.

*Ham.* Why did you laugh then, when I said 'man
delights not me'?

*Ros.* To think, my lord, if you delight not in man,
what 305
lenten entertainment the players shall receive
from you:
we coted them on the way; and hither are they
coming, to
offer you service.

*Ham.* He that plays the king shall be welcome; his
majesty shall have tribute of me; the adventurous
knight 310
shall use his foil and target; the lover shall not sigh
gratis;
the humourous man shall end his part in peace; the
clown
shall make those laugh whose lungs are tickled o'
the sere,
and the lady shall say her mind freely, or the blank
verse
shall halt for't. What players are they? 315

*Ros.* Even those you were wont to take such
delight
in, the tragedians of the city.

*Ham.* How chances it they travel? their residence,
both in reputation and profit, was better both ways.

*Ros.* I think their inhibition comes by the means of
the 320
late innovation.

*Ham.* Do they hold the same estimation they
did when
I was in the city? are they so followed?

*Ros.* No, indeed, are they not.

*Ham.* How comes it? do they grow rusty? 325

*Ros.* Nay, their endeavour keeps in the wonted
pace:

but there is, sir, an eyrie of children, little eyases,
that cry

out on the top of question and are most tyranically
clapped

for't: these are now the fashion, and so berattle the
common

stages—so they call them—that many wearing
rapiers 330

are afraid of goose-quills, and dare scarce come
thither.

*Ham.* What, are they children? who maintains 'em?
how are they escoted? Will they pursue the
quality no

longer than they can sing? will they not say after-
wards, if

they should grow themselves to common players,
—as it is 335

most like, if their means are no better,—their
writers do them

wrong, to make them exclaim against their own
succession?

*Ros.* Faith, there has been much to do on both
sides,

and the nation holds it no sin to tarre them to con-
troversy:

there was for a while no money bid for argument
unless 340

the poet and the player went to cuffs in the
question.

*Ham.* Is't possible?

*Guil.* O, there has been much throwing about of
brains.

*Ham.* Do the boys carry it away?

*Ros.* Ay, that they do, my lord; Hercules and his
load too. 345

*Ham.* It is not very strange; for my uncle is king of
Denmark, and those that would make mows at him
while

my father lived, give twenty, forty, fifty, a hundred
ducats

a-piece, for his picture in little. 'Sblood, there is
something

in this more than natural, if philosophy could find
    it out. 350

(*Flourish of trumpets within.*)

GUIL. There are the players.
HAM. Gentlemen, you are welcome to Elsinore.
    Your
hands, come then: the appurtenance of welcome is
    fashion
and ceremony: let me comply with you in this
    garb, lest
my extent to the players, which, I tell you, must
    show 355
fairly outwards, should more appear like enter-
    tainment
than yours. You are welcome: but my
    uncle-father and
aunt-mother are deceived.
GUIL. In what, my dear lord?
HAM. I am but mad north-north-west: when the
    wind 360
is southerly I know a hawk from a handsaw.

(*ENTER POLONIUS.*)

POL. Well be with you, gentlemen!
HAM. Hark you, Guildenstern; and you too: at each
ear a hearer: that great baby you see there is not
    yet out
of his swaddling clouts. 365
ROS. Happily he's the second time come to
    them; for
they say an old man is twice a child.
HAM. I will prophesy he comes to tell me of the
players; mark it. You say right, sir: o'Monday
    morning;
'twas so, indeed. 370
POL. My lord, I have news to tell you.
HAM. My lord, I have news to tell you. When
    Roscius
was an actor in Rome,—

*Pol.* The actors are come hither, my lord.
*Ham.* Buz, buz! 375
*Pol.* Upon my honour,—
*Ham.* Then came each actor on his ass,—
*Pol.* The best actors in the world, either for
    tragedy,
comedy, history, pastoral, pastoral-comical, histori-
    cal-pastoral,
tragical-historical, tragical-comical-historical-pas-
    toral, 380
scene individable, or poem unlimited: Seneca
    cannot be too
heavy, nor Plautus too light. For the law of writ
    and the
liberty these are the only men.
*Ham.* O Jephthah, judge of Israel, what a treasure
hadst thou! 385
*Pol.* What a treasure had he, my lord?
*Ham.* Why,
'One fair daughter, and no more,
The which he loved passing well.'
*Pol.* *(Aside)* Still on my daughter. 390
*Ham.* Am I not i' the right, old Jephthah?
*Pol.* If you call me Jephthah, my lord, I have a
    daughter
that I love passing well.
*Ham.* Nay, that follows not.
*Pol.* What follows, then, my lord? 395
*Ham.* Why,
'As by lot, God wot,'
and then, you know,
'It came to pass, as most like it was,'—
the first row of the pious chanson will show you
    more; 400
for look, where my abridgement comes.

*(Enter four or five Players.)*

You are welcome, masters; welcome, all. I am glad
    to see
thee well. Welcome, good friends. O, my old
    friend! Why

thy face is valanced since I saw thee last; comest
    thou to
beard me in Denmark? What, my young lady and
    mistress! 405
By'r lady, your ladyship is nearer to heaven than
when I saw you last, by the altitude of a chopine.
    Pray
God, your voice, like a piece of uncurrent gold,
    be not
cracked within the ring. Masters, you are all
    welcome.
We'll e'en to 't like French falconers, fly at any
    thing we 410
see: we'll have a speech straight: come, give us a
    taste of
your quality; come, a passionate speech.
FIRST PLAY. What speech, my good lord?
HAM. I heard thee speak me a speech once, but
    it was
never acted; or, if it was, not above once; for the
    play, I remember,415
pleased not the million; 'twas caviare to the
    general:
but it was—as I received it, and others, whose
    judgements
in such matters cried in the top of mine—an excel-
    lent play,
well digested in the scenes, set down with as much
    modesty
as cunning. I remember, one said there were no sal-
    lets in 420
the lines to make the matter savoury, nor no matter
    in the
phrase that might indict the author of affection; but
    called
it an honest method, as wholesome as sweet, and
    by very
much more handsome than fine. One speech in it I
    chiefly
loved: 'twas Æneas' tale to Dido; and thereabout of
    it especially, 425
where he speaks of Priam's slaughter: if it live in

your memory, begin at this line; let me see, let
    me see;
'The rugged Pyrrhus, like th' Hyrcanian beast,'—
It is not so: it begins with 'Pyrrhus.'
'The rugged Pyrrhus, he whose sable arms, 430
Black as his purpose, did the night resemble
When he lay couched in the ominous horse,
Hath now this dread and black complexion
    smear'd
With heraldry more dismal: head to foot
Now is he total gules; horridly trick'd 435
With blood of fathers, mothers, daughters, sons,
Baked and impasted with the parching streets,
That lend a tyrannous and a damned light
To their lord's murder: roasted in wrath and fire,
And thus o'er-sized with coagulate gore, 440
With eyes like carbuncles, the hellish Pyrrhus
Old grandsire Priam seeks.'
So, proceed you.
*Pol.* 'Fore God, my lord, well spoken, with good
    accent
and good discretion. 445
*First Play.* 'Anon he finds him
Striking too short at Greeks; his antique sword,
Rebellious to his arm, lies where it falls,
Repugnant to command: unequal match'd,
Pyrrhus at Priam drives; in rage strikes wide; 450
But with the whiff and wind of his fell sword
The unnerved father falls. Then senseless Ilium,
Seeming to feel this blow, with flaming top
Stoops to his base, and with a hideous crash
Takes prisoner Pyrrhus' ear: for, lo! his sword, 455
Which was declining on the milky head
Of reverend Priam, seem'd i' the air to stick:
So, as a painted tyrant, Pyrrhus stood.
And like a neutral to his will and matter,
Did nothing. 460
But as we often see, against some storm,
A silence in the heavens, the rack stand still,
The bold winds speechless and the orb below
As hush as death, anon the dreadful thunder
Doth rend the region, so after Pyrrhus' pause 465

Aroused vengeance sets him new a-work;
And never did the Cyclops' hammers fall
On Mars's armour, forged for proof eterne,
With less remorse than Pyrrhus' bleeding sword
Now falls on Priam. 470
Out, out, thou strumpet, Fortune! All you gods,
In general synod take away her power,
Break all the spokes and fellies from her wheel,
And bowl the round nave down the hill of heaven
As low as to the fiends!' 475
POL. This is too long.
HAM. It shall to the barber's, with your beard.
    Prithee,
say on: he's for a jig or a tale of bawdry, or he
    sleeps:
say on: come to Hecuba.
FIRST PLAY. 'But who, O, who had seen the mobled
    queen—' 480
HAM. 'The mobled queen?'
POL. That's good; 'mobled queen' is good.
FIRST PLAY. 'Run barefoot up and down, threat-
    ening the flames
With bisson rheum; a clout upon that head
Where late the diadem stood; and for a robe, 485
About her lank and all o'er-teemed loins,
A blanket, in the alarm of fear caught up:
Who this had seen, with tongue in venom steep'd
'Gainst Fortune's state would treason have pro-
    nounced:
But if the gods themselves did see her then, 490
When she saw Pyrrhus make malicious sport
In mincing with his sword her husband's limbs,
The instant burst of clamour that she made,
Unless things mortal move them not at all,
Would have made milch the burning eyes of
    heaven 495
And passion in the gods.'
POL. Look, whether he has not turned his
    colour and
has tears in's eyes. Prithee, no more.
HAM. 'Tis well; I'll have thee speak out the rest
    of this

soon. Good my lord, will you see the players well
bestowed? 500
Do you hear, let them be well used, for they are the
abstract
and brief chronicles of the time: after your death
you were
better have a bad epitaph than their ill report while
you live.
*Pol.* My lord, I will use them according to their
desert.
*Ham.* God's bodykins, man, much better: use
every 505
man after his desert, and who shall 'scape whip-
ping? Use
them after your own honour and dignity: the less
they deserve,
the more merit is in your bounty. Take them in.
*Pol.* Come, sirs.
*Ham.* Follow him, friends: we'll hear a play
to-morrow. 510

*(Exit Polonius with all the Players but the First.)*

Dost thou hear me, old friend; can you play the
Murder of
Gonzago?
*First Play.* Ay, my lord.
*Ham.* We'll ha't to-morrow night. You could, for a
need, study a speech of some dozen or sixteen
lines, which 515
I would set down and insert in't, could you not?
*First Play.* Ay, my lord.
*Ham.* Very well. Follow that lord; and look you
mock him not. *(Exit First Player.)* My good friends,
I'll
leave you till night: you are welcome to Elsinore.

520
*Ros.* Good my lord!
*Ham.* Ay, so, God be wi' ye! *(Exeunt Rosencrantz and
Guildenstern.)* Now I am alone.
O, what a rogue and peasant slave am I!
Is it not monstrous that this player here,

But in a fiction, in a dream of passion, 525
Could force his soul so to his own conceit
That from her working all his visage wann'd;
Tears in his eyes, distraction in's aspect,
A broken voice, and his whole function suiting
With forms to his conceit? and all for nothing! 530
For Hecuba!
What's Hecuba to him, or he to Hecuba,
That he should weep for her? What would he do,
Had he the motive and the cue for passion
That I have? He would drown the stage with
      tears 535
And cleave the general ear with horrid speech,
Make mad the guilty and appal the free,
Confound the ignorant, and amaze indeed
The very faculties of eyes and ears.
Yet I, 540
A dull and muddy-mettled rascal, peak,
Like John-a-dreams, unpregnant of my cause,
And can say nothing; no, not for a king,
Upon whose property and most dear life
A damn'd defeat was made. Am I a coward? 545
Who calls me villain? breaks my pate across?
Plucks off my beard, and blows it in my face?
Tweaks me by the nose? gives me the lie i' the
      throat,
As deep as to the lungs? who does me this?
Ha! 550
'Swounds, I should take it: for it cannot be
But I am pigeon-liver'd and lack gall
To make oppression bitter, or ere this
I should have fatted all the region kites
With this slave's offal: bloody, bawdy villain! 555
Remorseless, treacherous, lecherous, kindless
      villain!
O, vengeance!
Why, what an ass am I! This is most brave,
That I, the son of a dear father murder'd,
Prompted to my revenge by heaven and hell, 560
Must, like a whore, unpack my heart with words,
And fall a-cursing, like a very drab,
A scullion!

Fie upon't! foh! About, my brain! Hum, I have
    heard
That guilty creatures, sitting at a play, 565
Have by the very cunning of the scene
Been struck so to the soul that presently
They have proclaim'd their malefactions;
For murder, though it have no tongue, will speak
With most miraculous organ. I'll have these
    players 570
Play something like the murder of my father
Before mine uncle: I'll observe his looks;
I'll tent him to the quick: if he but blench,
I know my course. The spirit that I have seen
May be the devil; and the devil hath power 575
To assume a pleasing shape; yea, and perhaps
Out of my weakness and my melancholy,
As he is very potent with such spirits,
Abuses me to damn me. I'll have grounds
More relative than this. The play's the thing 580
Wherein I'll catch the conscience of the king. *(Exit.)*

# ACT III

## SCENE I. A ROOM IN THE CASTLE.

*(Enter King, Queen, Polonius, Ophelia, Rosencrantz, and Guildenstern.)*

*King.* And can you, by no drift of circumstance,
Get from him why he puts on this confusion,
Grating so harshly all his days of quiet
With turbulent and dangerous lunacy?
*Ros.* He does confess he feels himself distracted, 5
But from what cause he will by no means speak.
*Guil.* Nor do we find him forward to be sounded;
But, with a crafty madness, keeps aloof,
When we would bring him on to some confession
Of his true state.
*Queen.* Did he receive you well? 10
*Ros.* Most like a gentleman.
*Guil.* But with much forcing of his disposition.
*Ros.* Niggard of question, but of our demands
Most free in his reply.
*Queen.* Did you assay him
To any pastime? 15
*Ros.* Madam, it so fell out that certain players
We o'er-raught on the way: of these we told him,
And there did seem in him a kind of joy
To hear of it: they are about the court,
And, as I think, they have already order 20

This night to play before him.
*POL.* 'Tis most true:
And he beseech'd me to entreat your majesties
To hear and see the matter.
*KING.* With all my heart; and it doth much
    content me
To hear him so inclined. ₂₅
Good gentlemen, give him a further edge,
And drive his purpose on to these delights.
*ROS.* We shall, my lord.

        *(Exeunt Rosencrantz and Guildenstern.)*

*KING.* Sweet Gertrude, leave us too;
For we have closely sent for Hamlet hither,
That he, as 'twere by accident, may here ₃₀
Affront Ophelia:
Her father and myself, lawful espials,
Will so bestow ourselves that, seeing unseen,
We may of their encounter frankly judge,
And gather by him, as he is behaved, ₃₅
If't be the affliction of his love or no
That thus he suffers for.
*QUEEN.* I shall obey you:
And for your part, Ophelia, I do wish
That your good beauties be the happy cause
Of Hamlet's wildness: so shall I hope your
    virtues ₄₀
Will bring him to his wonted way again,
To both your honours.
*OPH.* Madam, I wish it may. *(Exit Queen.)*
*POL.* Ophelia, walk you here. Gracious, so
    please you,
We will bestow ourselves. *(To Ophelia)* Read on this
    book;
That show of such an exercise may colour ₄₅
Your loneliness. We are oft to blame in this,—
'Tis too much proved—that with devotion's
    visage
And pious action we do sugar o'er
The devil himself.
*KING. (Aside)* O, 'tis too true!

How smart a lash that speech doth give my con-
 science! 50
The harlot's cheek, beautied with plastering art,
Is not more ugly to the thing that helps it
Than is my deed to my most painted word:
O heavy burthen!
*Pol.* I hear him coming: let's withdraw, my lord. 55

     *(Exeunt King and Polonius.)*

    *(Enter Hamlet.)*

*Ham.* To be, or not to be: that is the question:
Whether 'tis nobler in the mind to suffer
The slings and arrows of outrageous fortune,
Or to take arms against a sea of troubles,
And by opposing end them? To die: to sleep; 60
No more; and by a sleep to say we end
The heart-ache, and the thousand natural shocks
That flesh is heir to, 'tis a consummation
Devoutly to be wish'd. To die, to sleep;
To sleep: perchance to dream: ay, there's the rub; 65
For in that sleep of death what dreams may come,
When we have shuffled off this mortal coil,
Must give us pause: there's the respect
That makes calamity of so long life;
For who would bear the whips and scorns of
 time, 70
The oppressor's wrong, the proud man's
 contumely,
The pangs of despised love, the law's delay,
The insolence of office, and the spurns
That patient merit of the unworthy takes,
When he himself might his quietus make 75
With a bare bodkin? who would fardels bear,
To grunt and sweat under a weary life,
But that the dread of something after death,
The undiscover'd country from whose bourn
No traveller returns, puzzles the will, 80
And makes us rather bear those ills we have
Than fly to others that we know not of?
Thus conscience does make cowards of us all,

And thus the native hue of resolution
Is sicklied o'er with the pale cast of thought, 85
And enterprises of great pitch and moment
With this regard their currents turn awry
And lose the name of action. Soft you now!
The fair Ophelia! Nymph, in thy orisons
Be all my sins remember'd.

*Oph.* Good my lord, 90
How does your honour for this many a day?

*Ham.* I humbly thank you: well, well, well.

*Oph.* My lord, I have remembrances of yours,
That I have longed long to re-deliver;
I pray you, now receive them.

*Ham.* No, not I; 95
I never gave you aught.

*Oph.* My honour'd lord, you know right well
      you did;
And with them words of so sweet breath composed
As made the things more rich: their perfume lost,
Take these again; for to the noble mind 100
Rich gifts wax poor when givers prove unkind.
There, my lord.

*Ham.* Ha, ha! are you honest?

*Oph.* My lord?

*Ham.* Are you fair? 105

*Oph.* What means your lordship?

*Ham.* That if you be honest and fair, your honesty
should admit no discourse to your beauty.

*Oph.* Could beauty, my lord, have better commerce
than with honesty? 110

*Ham.* Ay, truly; for the power of beauty will sooner
transform honesty from what it is to a bawd than
      the force
of honesty can translate beauty into his likeness:
      this was
sometime a paradox, but now the time gives it
      proof. I
did love you once. 115

*Oph.* Indeed, my lord, you made me believe so.

*Ham.* You should not have believed me; for virtue
cannot so inoculate our old stock but we shall
      relish of it:

I loved you not.

*Oph.* I was the more deceived. 120

*Ham.* Get thee to a nunnery: why wouldst thou be a
breeder of sinners? I am myself indifferent honest; but yet
I could accuse me of such things that it were better my
mother had not borne me: I am very proud, re-vengeful,
ambitious; with more offences at my beck than I have 125
thoughts to put them in, imagination to give them shape,
or time to act them in. What should such fellows as I do
crawling between heaven and earth? We are arrant knaves
all; believe none of us. Go thy ways to a nunnery.
Where's your father? 130

*Oph.* At home, my lord.

*Ham.* Let the doors be shut upon him, that he may
play the fool no where but in's own house.
Farewell.

*Oph.* O, help him, you sweet heavens!

*Ham.* If thou dost marry, I'll give thee this plague for 135
thy dowry: be thou as chaste as ice, as pure as snow, thou
shalt not escape calumny. Get thee to a nunnery, go: farewell.
Or, if thou wilt needs marry, marry a fool; for wise
men know well enough what monsters you make of them.
To a nunnery, go; and quickly too. Farewell. 140

*Oph.* O heavenly powers, restore him!

*Ham.* I have heard of your paintings too, well enough;
God hath given you one face, and you make yourselves
another: you jig, you amble, and you lisp, and nick-name

God's creatures, and make your wantonness your
   ignorance. 145
Go to, I'll no more on't; it hath made me mad.
I say, we will have no more marriages: those that
   are married
already, all but one, shall live; the rest shall keep as
they are. To a nunnery, go. *(Exit.)*
*OPH.* O, what a noble mind is here o'erthrown! 150
The courtier's, soldier's, scholar's, eye, tongue,
   sword:
The expectancy and rose of the fair state,
The glass of fashion and the mould of form,
The observed of all observers, quite, quite down!
And I, of ladies most deject and wretched, 155
That suck'd the honey of his music vows,
Now see that noble and most sovereign reason,
Like sweet bells jangled, out of tune and harsh;
That unmatch'd form and feature of blown youth
Blasted with ecstasy: O, woe is me, 160
To have seen what I have seen, see what I see!

*(RE-ENTER KING AND POLONIUS.)*

*KING.* Love! his affections do not that way tend;
Nor what he spake, though it lack'd form a little,
Was not like madness. There's something in
   his soul
O'er which his melancholy sits on brood, 165
And I do doubt the hatch and the disclose
Will be some danger: which for to prevent,
I have in quick determination
Thus set it down:—he shall with speed to England,
For the demand of our neglected tribute: 170
Haply the seas and countries different
With variable objects shall expel
This something-settled matter in his heart,
Whereon his brains still beating puts him thus
From fashion of himself. What think you on 't? 175
*POL.* It shall do well: but yet do I believe
The origin and commencement of his grief
Sprung from neglected love. How now, Ophelia!
You need not tell us what Lord Hamlet said;

We heard it all. My lord, do as you please; 180
But, if you hold it fit, after the play,
Let his queen mother all alone entreat him
To show his grief: let her be round with him;
And I'll be placed, so please you, in the ear
Of all their conference. If she find him not, 185
To England send him, or confine him where
Your wisdom best shall think.
*KING.* It shall be so:
Madness in great ones must not unwatch'd go.
*(Exeunt.)*

## SCENE II. A HALL IN THE CASTLE

*(Enter Hamlet and Players.)*

*HAM.* Speak the speech, I pray you, as I pro-
nounced
it to you, trippingly on the tongue: but if you
mouth it, as
many of your players do, I had as lief the town-
crier spoke
my lines. Nor do not saw the air too much
with your
hand, thus; but use all gently: for in the very tor-
rent, tempest, 5
and, as I may say, whirlwind of your passion, you
must acquire and beget a temperance that may
give it
smoothness. O, it offends me to the soul to hear a
robustious
periwig-pated fellow tear a passion to tatters,
to very
rags, to split the ears of the groundlings, who, for
the most 10
part, are capable of nothing but inexplicable dumb-
shows
and noise: I would have such a fellow whipped for
o'er-doing
Termagant; it out-herods Herod: pray you,
avoid it.
*FIRST PLAY.* I warrant your honour.

*Ham.* Be not too tame neither, but let your own discretion 15
be your tutor: suit the action to the word, the word
to the action; with this special observance, that you
   o'er-step
not the modesty of nature: for any thing so
   overdone
is from the purpose of playing, whose end, both at
   the first
and now, was and is, to hold, as 'twere, the mirror
   up to 20
nature; to show virtue her own feature, scorn
   her own
image, and the very age and body of the time his
   form and
pressure. Now this overdone or come tardy off,
   though
it make the unskilful laugh, cannot but make the
   judicious
grieve; the censure of the which one must in your
   allowance 25
o'erweigh a whole theatre of others. O, there be
players that I have seen play, and heard others
   praise, and
that highly, not to speak it profanely, that neither
   having
the accent of Christians nor the gait of Christian,
   pagan,
nor man, have so strutted and bellowed, that I have
   thought 30
some of nature's journeymen had made men, and
   not made
them well, they imitated humanity so abominably.
*First Play.* I hope we have reformed that indif-
   ferently
with us, sir.
*Ham.* O, reform it altogether. And let those that
   play 35
your clowns speak no more than is set down for
   them: for
there be of them that will themselves laugh, to set
   on some

quantity of barren spectators to laugh too, though
   in the
mean time some necessary question of the play be
   then to
be considered: that's villanous, and shows a most
   pitiful ambition 40
in the fool that uses it. Go, make you ready.

*(Exeunt Players.)*

*(ENTER POLONIUS, ROSENCRANTZ, AND GUILDENSTERN.)*

How now, my lord! will the king hear this piece of
   work?
*POL.* And the queen too, and that presently.
*HAM.* Bid the players make haste. *(Exit Polonius.)*
Will you two help to hasten them? 45
*ROS. GUIL.* We will, my lord.

*(Exeunt Rosencrantz and Guildenstern.)*

*HAM.* What ho! Horatio!

*(ENTER HORATIO.)*

*HOR.* Here, sweet lord, at your service.
*HAM.* Horatio, thou art e'en as just a man
As e'er my conversation coped withal. 50
*HOR.* O, my dear lord,—
*HAM.* Nay, do not think I flatter;
For what advancement may I hope from thee,
That no revenue hast but thy good spirits,
To feed and clothe thee? Why should the poor be
   flatter'd?
No, let the candied tongue lick absurd pomp, 55
And crook the pregnant hinges of the knee
Where thrift may follow fawning. Dost thou hear?
Since my dear soul was mistress of her choice,
And could of men distinguish, her election
Hath seal'd thee for herself: for thou hast been 60
As one, in suffering all, that suffers nothing;
A man that fortune's buffets and rewards

Hast ta'en with equal thanks: and blest are those
Whose blood and judgement are so well com-
    mingled
That they are not a pipe for fortune's finger 65
To sound what stop she please. Give me that man
That is not passion's slave, and I will wear him
In my heart's core, ay, in my heart of heart,
As I do thee. Something too much of this.
There is a play to-night before the king; 70
One scene of it comes near the circumstance
Which I have told thee of my father's death:
I prithee, when thou seest that act a-foot,
Even with the very comment of thy soul
Observe my uncle: if his occulted guilt 75
Do not itself unkennel in one speech,
It is a damned ghost that we have seen,
And my imaginations are as foul
As Vulcan's stithy. Give him heedful note;
For I mine eyes will rivet to his face, 80
And after we will both our judgements join
In censure of his seeming.
HOR. Well, my lord:
If he steal aught the whilst this play is playing,
And 'scape detecting, I will pay the theft.
HAM. They are coming to the play: I must be idle; 85
Get you a place.

*(Danish march. A flourish. Enter KING, QUEEN, POLONIUS,
OPHELIA, ROSENCRANTZ, GUILDENSTERN, and other Lords
    attendant, with the Guard carrying torches.)*

KING. How fares our cousin Hamlet?
HAM. Excellent, i' faith; of the chameleon's dish:
    I eat
the air, promise-crammed: you cannot feed
    capons so.
KING. I have nothing with this answer, Hamlet;
    these 90
words are not mine.
HAM. No, nor mine now. *(To Polonius)* My
    lord, you
played once i' the university, you say?

*Pol.* That did I, my lord, and was accounted
    a good
actor. 95
*Ham.* What did you enact?
*Pol.* I did enact Julius Cæsar: I was killed i' the
    Capitol;
Brutus killed me.
*Ham.* It was a brute part of him to kill so capital a
calf there. Be the players ready? 100
*Ros.* Ay, my lord; they stay upon your patience.
*Queen.* Come hither, my dear Hamlet, sit by me.
*Ham.* No, good mother, here's metal more at-
    tractive.
*Pol.* *(To the King)* O, ho! do you mark that?
*Ham.* Lady, shall I lie in your lap? 105

                *(Lying down at Ophelia's feet.)*

*Oph.* No, my lord.
*Ham.* I mean, my head upon your lap?
*Oph.* Ay, my lord.
*Ham.* Do you think I meant country matters?
*Oph.* I think nothing, my lord. 110
*Ham.* That's a fair thought to lie between maids'
    legs.
*Oph.* What is, my lord?
*Ham.* Nothing.
*Oph.* You are merry, my lord.
*Ham.* Who, I? 115
*Oph.* Ay, my lord.
*Ham.* O God, your only jig-maker. What should a
man do but be merry? for, look you, how cheerfully
    my
mother looks, and my father died within 's two
    hours.
*Oph.* Nay, 'tis twice two months, my lord. 120
*Ham.* So long? Nay, then, let the devil wear
    black, for
I'll have a suit of sables. O heavens! die two
    months ago,
and not forgotten yet? Then there's hope a great
    man's

memory may outlive his life half a year: but, by'r
    lady, he
must build churches then; or else shall he suffer not
    thinking ₁₂₅
on, with the hobby-horse, whose epitaph is,
    'For, O,
for, O, the hobby-horse is forgot.'

*(Hautboys play. The dumb-show enters.)*

*(Enter a King and a Queen very lovingly; the Queen embracing
him, and he her. She kneels, and makes show of protestation
unto him. He takes her up, and declines his head upon her neck:
lays him down upon a bank of flowers: she, seeing him asleep,
leaves him. Anon comes in a fellow, takes off his crown, kisses it,
and pours poison in the King's ears, and exit. The Queen returns; finds the King dead, and makes passionate action. The
Poisoner, with some two or three Mutes, comes in again,
seeming to lament with her. The dead body is carried away. The
Poisoner wooes the Queen with gifts: she seems loath and un-
willing awhile, but in the end accepts his love.)*

*(Exeunt.)*

OPH. What means this, my lord?
HAM. Marry, this is miching mallecho; it means
    mischief. ₁₃₀
OPH. Belike this show imports the argument of the
    play.

*(Enter Prologue.)*

HAM. We shall know by this fellow: the players
    cannot
keep counsel; they'll tell all.
OPH. Will he tell us what this show meant?
HAM. Ay, or any show that you'll show him: be not
    you ₁₃₅
ashamed to show, he'll not shame to tell you what
    it means.
OPH. You are naught, you are naught: I'll mark the
    play.

*Pro.* For us, and for our tragedy,
Here stooping to your clemency, 140
We beg your hearing patiently.
*Ham.* Is this a prologue, or the posy of a ring?
*Oph.* 'Tis brief, my lord.
*Ham.* As woman's love.

*(Enter two Players, King and Queen.)*

*P. King.* Full thirty times hath Phœbus' cart gone
    round 145
Neptune's salt wash and Tellus' orbed ground,
And thirty dozen moons with borrowed sheen
About the world have times twelve thirties been,
Since love our hearts and Hymen did our hands
Unite commutual in most sacred bands. 150
*P. Queen.* So many journeys may the sun
    and moon
Make us again count o'er ere love be done!
But, woe is me, you are so sick of late,
So far from cheer and from your former state,
That I distrust you. Yet, though I distrust, 155
Discomfort you, my lord, it nothing must:
For women's fear and love holds quantity,
In neither aught, or in extremity.
Now, what my love is, proof hath made you know,
And as my love is sized, my fear is so: 160
Where love is great, the littlest doubts are fear,
Where little fears grow great, great love grows
    there.
*P. King.* Faith, I must leave thee, love, and shortly
    too;
My operant powers their functions leave to do:
And thou shalt live in this fair world behind, 165
Honour'd, beloved; and haply one as kind
For husband shalt thou—
*P. Queen.* O, confound the rest!
Such love must needs be treason in my breast:
In second husband let me be accurst!
None wed the second but who kill'd the first. 170
*Ham. (Aside)* Wormwood, wormwood.
*P. Queen.* The instances that second marriage

move

Are base respects of thrift, but none of love:

A second time I kill my husband dead,

When second husband kisses me in bed. 175

P. KING. I do believe you think what now you
  speak,

But what we do determine oft we break.

Purpose is but the slave to memory,

Of violent birth but poor validity:

Which now, like fruit unripe, sticks on the tree, 180

But fall unshaken when they mellow be.

Most necessary 'tis that we forget

To pay ourselves what to ourselves is debt:

What to ourselves in passion we propose,

The passion ending, doth the purpose lose. 185

The violence of either grief or joy

Their own enactures with themselves destroy:

Where joy most revels, grief doth most lament;

Grief joys, joy grieves, on slender accident.

This world is not for aye, nor 'tis not strange 190

That even our loves should with our fortunes
  change,

For 'tis a question left us yet to prove,

Whether love lead fortune or else fortune love.

The great man down, you mark his favourite flies;

The poor advanced makes friends of enemies: 195

And hitherto doth love on fortune tend;

For who not needs shall never lack a friend,

And who in want a hollow friend doth try

Directly seasons him his enemy.

But, orderly to end where I begun, 200

Our wills and fates do so contrary run,

That our devices still are overthrown,

Our thoughts are ours, their ends none of our own:

So think thou wilt no second husband wed,

But die thy thoughts when thy first lord is dead. 205

P. QUEEN. Nor earth to me give food nor heaven
  light!

Sport and repose lock from me day and night!

To desperation turn my trust and hope!

An anchor's cheer in prison be my scope!

Each opposite, that blanks the face of joy, 210

Meet what I would have well and it destroy!
Both here and hence pursue me lasting strife,
If, once a widow, ever I be wife!
*HAM.* If she should break it now!
*P. KING.* 'Tis deeply sworn. Sweet, leave me here
    awhile; $_{215}$
My spirits grow dull, and fain I would beguile
The tedious day with sleep. *(Sleeps.)*
*P. QUEEN.* Sleep rock thy brain;
And never come mischance between us twain!
    *(Exit.)*
*HAM.* Madam, how like you this play?
*QUEEN.* The lady doth protest too much, methinks.
  $_{220}$
*HAM.* O, but she'll keep her word.
*KING.* Have you heard the argument? Is there no
offence in't?
*HAM.* No, no, they do but jest, poison in jest; no
    offence
i' the world. $_{225}$
*KING.* What do you call the play?
*HAM.* The Mouse-trap. Marry, how? Tropically.
This play is the image of a murder done in Vienna:
    Gonzago
is the duke's name; his wife, Baptista: you shall see
anon; 'tis a knavish piece of work: but what o' that?
    your $_{230}$
majesty, and we that have free souls, it touches us
    not: let
the galled jade wince, our withers are unwrung.

*(ENTER LUCIANUS.)*

This is one Lucianus, nephew to the king.
*OPH.* You are as good as a chorus, my lord.
*HAM.* I could interpret between you and your love,
    if $_{235}$
I could see the puppets dallying.
*OPH.* You are keen, my lord, you are keen.
*HAM.* It would cost you a groaning to take off my
    edge.
*OPH.* Still better, and worse.

*Ham.* So you must take your husbands. Begin, mur-
     derer; 240
pox, leave thy damnable faces, and begin. Come:
the croaking raven doth bellow for revenge.
*Luc.* Thoughts black, hands apt, drugs fit, and time
     agreeing;
Confederate season, else no creature seeing;
Thou mixture rank, of midnight weeds collected,

245
With Hecate's ban thrice blasted, thrice infected,
Thy natural magic and dire property,
On wholesome life usurp immediately.

(*Pours the poison into the sleeper's ear.*)

*Ham.* He poisons him i' the garden for his
     estate. His
name's Gonzago: the story is extant, and written in
     very 250
choice Italian: you shall see anon how the murderer
     gets
the love of Gonzago's wife.
*Oph.* The king rises.
*Ham.* What, frighted with false fire!
*Queen.* How fares my lord? 255
*Pol.* Give o'er the play.
*King.* Give me some light. Away!
*Pol.* Lights, lights, lights!

(*Exeunt all but Hamlet and Horatio.*)

*Ham.* Why, let the stricken deer go weep,
The hart ungalled play; 260
For some must watch, while some must sleep:
Thus runs the world away.
Would not this, sir, and a forest of feathers—if the
     rest of
my fortunes turn Turk with me—with two Pro-
     vincial roses
on my razed shoes, get me a fellowship in a cry of
     players, 265
sir?

*Hor.* Half a share.

*Ham.* A whole one, I.

For thou dost know, O Damon dear,

This realm dismantled was 270

Of Jove himself; and now reigns here

A very, very—pajock.

*Hor.* You might have rhymed.

*Ham.* O good Horatio, I'll take the ghost's word
    for a

thousand pound. Didst perceive? 275

*Hor.* Very well, my lord.

*Ham.* Upon the talk of the poisoning?

*Hor.* I did very well note him.

*Ham.* Ah, ha! Come, some music! come, the
    recorders! 280

For if the king like not the comedy,

Why then, belike, he likes it not, perdy.

Come, some music!

(*Re-enter Rosencrantz and Guildenstern.*)

*Guil.* Good my lord, vouchsafe me a word
    with you.

*Ham.* Sir, a whole history. 285

*Guil.* The king, sir,—

*Ham.* Ay, sir, what of him?

*Guil.* Is in his retirement marvellous distempered.

*Ham.* With drink, sir?

*Guil.* No, my lord, rather with choler. 290

*Ham.* Your wisdom should show itself more
    richer to

signify this to the doctor; for, for me to put him to
    his purgation

would perhaps plunge him into far more choler.

*Guil.* Good my lord, put your discourse into some

frame, and start not so wildly from my affair. 295

*Ham.* I am tame, sir: pronounce.

*Guil.* The queen, your mother, in most great af-
    fliction

of spirit, hath sent me to you.

*Ham.* You are welcome.

*Guil.* Nay, good my lord, this courtesy is not of

the $_{300}$

right breed. If it shall please you to make me a wholesome

answer, I will do your mother's commandment: if not, your

pardon and my return shall be the end of my business.

*Ham.* Sir, I cannot.

*Guil.* What, my lord? $_{305}$

*Ham.* Make you a wholesome answer; my wit's diseased:

but, sir, such answer as I can make, you shall command;

or rather, as you say, my mother: therefore no

more, but to the matter: my mother, you say,—

*Ros.* Then thus she says; your behaviour hath struck $_{310}$

her into amazement and admiration.

*Ham.* O wonderful son, that can so astonish a mother!

But is there no sequel at the heels of this mother's admiration?

Impart.

*Ros.* She desires to speak with you in her closet, ere $_{315}$

you go to bed.

*Ham.* We shall obey, were she ten times our mother.

Have you any further trade with us?

*Ros.* My lord, you once did love me.

*Ham.* So I do still, by these pickers and stealers. $_{320}$

*Ros.* Good my lord, what is your cause of distemper?

you do surely bar the door upon your own liberty, if you

deny your griefs to your friend.

*Ham.* Sir, I lack advancement.

*Ros.* How can that be, when you have the voice of the $_{325}$

king himself for your succession in Denmark?

*Ham.* Ay, sir, but 'while the grass grows,'—the proverb

is something musty.

*(Re-enter Players with recorders.)*

O, the recorders! let me see one. To withdraw with
    you:—
why do you go about to recover the wind of me, as
    if you ₃₃₀
would drive me into a toil?
*Guil.* O, my lord, if my duty be too bold, my
    love is
too unmannerly.
*Ham.* I do not well understand that. Will you play
upon this pipe? ₃₃₅
*Guil.* My lord, I cannot.
*Ham.* I pray you.
*Guil.* Believe me, I cannot.
*Ham.* I do beseech you.
*Guil.* I know no touch of it, my lord. ₃₄₀
*Ham.* It is as easy as lying: govern these ventages
with your fingers and thumb, give it breath
    with your
mouth, and it will discourse most eloquent
    music. Look
you, these are the stops.
*Guil.* But these cannot I command to any utterance
    ₃₄₅
of harmony; I have not the skill.
*Ham.* Why, look you now, how unworthy a
    thing you
make of me! You would play upon me; you
    would seem
to know my stops; you would pluck out the heart
    of my
mystery; you would sound me from my lowest
    note to the ₃₅₀
top of my compass: and there is much music, ex-
    cellent
voice, in this little organ; yet cannot you make it
    speak.
'Sblood, do you think I am easier to be played on
    than a
pipe? Call me what instrument you will, though
    you can

fret me, yet you cannot play upon me. 355

(*ENTER POLONIUS.*)

God bless you, sir!
*POL.* My lord, the queen would speak with
    you, and
presently.
*HAM.* Do you see yonder cloud that's almost in
    shape
of a camel? 360
*POL.* By the mass, and 'tis like a camel, indeed.
*HAM.* Methinks it is like a weasel.
*POL.* It is backed like a weasel.
*HAM.* Or like a whale?
*POL.* Very like a whale. 365
*HAM.* Then I will come to my mother by and by.
They fool me to the top of my bent. I will come
    by and
by.
*POL. I will say so. (Exit Polonius.)*
*HAM.* 'By and by' is easily said. Leave me, friends.
    370

(*Exeunt all but Hamlet.*)

'Tis now the very witching time of night,
When churchyards yawn, and hell itself breathes
    out
Contagion to this world: now could I drink hot
    blood,
And do such bitter business as the day
Would quake to look on. Soft! now to my
    mother. 375
O heart, lose not thy nature; let not ever
The soul of Nero enter this firm bosom:
Let me be cruel, not unnatural:
I will speak daggers to her, but use none;
My tongue and soul in this be hypocrites; 380
How in my words soever she be shent,
To give them seals never, my soul, consent! *(Exit.)*

## SCENE III. A ROOM IN THE CASTLE: (ENTER KING, ROSENCRANTZ, AND GUILDENSTERN.)

*KING.* I like him not, nor stands it safe with us
To let his madness range. Therefore prepare you;
I your commission will forthwith dispatch,
And he to England shall along with you:
The terms of our estate may not endure 5
Hazard so near us as doth hourly grow
Out of his lunacies.
*GUIL.* We will ourselves provide:
Most holy and religious fear it is
To keep those many bodies safe
That live and feed upon your majesty. 10
*ROS.* The single and peculiar life is bound
With all the strength and armour of the mind
To keep itself from noyance; but much more
That spirit upon whose weal depends and rests
The lives of many. The cease of majesty 15
Dies not alone, but like a gulf doth draw
What's near it with it: it is a massy wheel,
Fix'd on the summit of the highest mount,
To whose huge spokes ten thousand lesser things
Are mortised and adjoin'd; which, when it falls, 20
Each small annexment, petty consequence,
Attends the boisterous ruin. Never alone
Did the king sigh, but with a general groan.
*KING.* Arm you, I pray you, to this speedy voyage,
For we will fetters put about this fear, 25
Which now goes too free-footed.
*ROS.* } We will haste us.
*GUIL.*}

*(Exeunt Rosencrantz and Guildenstern.)*

*(ENTER POLONIUS.)*

*POL.* My lord, he's going to his mother's closet:
Behind the arras I'll convey myself,
To hear the process; I'll warrant she'll tax him
    home:
And, as you said, and wisely was it said, 30

'Tis meet that some more audience than a mother,
Since nature makes them partial, should o'erhear
The speech, of vantage. Fare you well, my liege:
I'll call upon you ere you go to bed,
And tell you what I know.
KING. Thanks, dear my lord. ₃₅

*(Exit Polonius.)*

O, my offence is rank, it smells to heaven;
It hath the primal eldest curse upon't,
A brother's murder. Pray can I not,
Though inclination be as sharp as will:
My stronger guilt defeats my strong intent, ₄₀
And like a man to double business bound,
I stand in pause where I shall first begin,
And both neglect. What if this cursed hand
Were thicker than itself with brother's blood,
Is there not rain enough in the sweet heavens ₄₅
To wash it white as snow? Whereto serves mercy
But to confront the visage of offence?
And what's in prayer but this twofold force,
To be forestalled ere we come to fall,
Or pardon'd being down? Then I'll look up; ₅₀
My fault is past. But O, what form of prayer
Can serve my turn? 'Forgive me my foul murder?'
That cannot be, since I am still possess'd
Of those effects for which I did the murder,
My crown, mine own ambition and my queen. ₅₅
May one be pardon'd and retain the offence?
In the corrupted currents of this world
Offence's gilded hand may shove by justice,
And oft 'tis seen the wicked prize itself
Buys out the law: but 'tis not so above; ₆₀
There is no shuffling, there the action lies
In his true nature, and we ourselves compell'd
Even to the teeth and forehead of our faults
To give in evidence. What then? what rests?
Try what repentance can: what can it not? ₆₅
Yet what can it when one can not repent?
O wretched state! O bosom black as death!
O limed soul, that struggling to be free

Art more engaged! Help, angels! make assay!
Bow, stubborn knees, and, heart with strings of
    steel, 70
Be soft as sinews of the new-born babe!
*All may be well. (Retires and kneels.)*

*(Enter Hamlet.)*

*Ham.* Now might I do it pat, now he is praying;
And now I'll do't: and so he goes to heaven:
And so am I revenged. That would be scann'd: 75
A villain kills my father; and for that,
I, his sole son, do this same villain send
To heaven.
O, this is hire and salary, not revenge.
He took my father grossly, full of bread, 80
With all his crimes broad blown, as flush as May;
And how his audit stands who knows save
    heaven?
But in our circumstance and course of thought,
'Tis heavy with him: and am I then revenged,
To take him in the purging of his soul, 85
When he is fit and season'd for his passage?
No.
Up, sword, and know thou a more horrid hent:
When he is drunk asleep, or in his rage,
Or in the incestuous pleasure of his bed; 90
At game, a-swearing, or about some act
That has no relish of salvation in 't;
Then trip him, that his heels may kick at heaven
And that his soul may be as damn'd and black
As hell, whereto it goes. My mother stays: 95
This physic but prolongs thy sickly days. *(Exit.)*
*King. (Rising)* My words fly up, my thoughts re-
    main below:
Words without thoughts never to heaven go. *(Exit.)*


SCENE IV. THE QUEEN'S CLOSET: (ENTER
QUEEN AND POLONIUS.)

*Pol.* He will come straight. Look you lay home
    to him:

Tell him his pranks have been too broad to bear
    with,
And that your grace hath screen'd and stood
    between
Much heat and him. I'll sconce me even here.
Pray you, be round with him.
*Ham. (Within)* Mother, mother, mother!₅
*Queen.* I'll warrant you; fear me not. Withdraw, I
hear him coming.

*(Polonius hides behind the arras.)*

*(Enter Hamlet.)*

*Ham.* Now, mother, what's the matter?
*Queen.* Hamlet, thou hast thy father much
    offended.
*Ham.* Mother, you have my father much offended.
¹⁰
*Queen.* Come, come, you answer with an idle
    tongue.
*Ham.* Go, go, you question with a wicked tongue.
*Queen.* Why, how now, Hamlet!
*Ham.* What's the matter now?
*Queen.* Have you forgot me?
*Ham.* No, by the rood, not so:
You are the queen, your husband's brother's
    wife; ₁₅
And—would it were not so!—you are my mother.
*Queen.* Nay, then, I'll set those to you that can
    speak.
*Ham.* Come, come, and sit you down; you shall not
    budge;
You go not till I set you up a glass
Where you may see the inmost part of you. ₂₀
*Queen.* What wilt thou do? thou wilt not
    murder me?
Help, help, ho!
*Pol. (Behind)* What, ho! help, help, help!
*Ham. (Drawing)* How now! a rat? Dead, for a ducat,
    dead!

*(Makes a pass through the arras.)*

POL. *(Behind)* O, I am slain! *(Falls and dies.)*
QUEEN. O me, what hast thou done? 25
HAM. Nay, I know not: is it the king?
QUEEN. O, what a rash and bloody deed is this!
HAM. A bloody deed! almost as bad, good mother,
As kill a king, and marry with his brother.
QUEEN. As kill a king!
HAM. Ay, lady, 'twas my word. 30

*(Lifts up the arras and discovers Polonius.)*

Thou wretched, rash, intruding fool, farewell!
I took thee for thy better: take thy fortune;
Thou find'st to be too busy is some danger.
Leave wringing of your hands: peace! sit you
     down,
And let me wring your heart: for so I shall, 35
If it be made of penetrable stuff;
If damned custom have not brass'd it so,
That it be proof and bulwark against sense.
QUEEN. What have I done, that thou darest wag thy
     tongue
In noise so rude against me?
HAM. Such an act 40
That blurs the grace and blush of modesty,
Calls virtue hypocrite, takes off the rose
From the fair forehead of an innocent love,
And sets a blister there; makes marriage vows
As false as dicers' oaths: O, such a deed 45
As from the body of contraction plucks
The very soul, and sweet religion makes
A rhapsody of words: heaven's face doth glow;
Yea, this solidity and compound mass,
With tristful visage, as against the doom,
Is thought-sick at the act. 50
QUEEN. Ay me, what act,
That roars so loud and thunders in the index?
HAM. Look here, upon this picture, and on this,
The counterfeit presentment of two brothers.
See what a grace was seated on this brow; 55

Hyperion's curls, the front of Jove himself,
An eye like Mars, to threaten and command;
A station like the herald Mercury
New-lighted on a heaven-kissing hill;
A combination and a form indeed, 60
Where every god did seem to set his seal
To give the world assurance of a man:
This was your husband. Look you now, what
    follows:
Here is your husband; like a mildew'd ear,
Blasting his wholesome brother. Have you eyes? 65
Could you on this fair mountain leave to feed,
And batten on this moor? Ha! have you eyes?
You cannot call it love, for at your age
The hey-day in the blood is tame, it's humble,
And waits upon the judgement: and what judge-
    ment 70
Would step from this to this? Sense sure you have,
Else could you not have motion: but sure that sense
Is apoplex'd: for madness would not err,
Nor sense to ecstasy was ne'er so thrall'd
But it reserved some quantity of choice, 75
To serve in such a difference. What devil was't
That thus hath cozen'd you at hoodman-blind?
Eyes without feeling, feeling without sight,
Ears without hands or eyes, smelling sans all,
Or but a sickly part of one true sense 80
Could not so mope.
O shame! where is thy blush? Rebellious hell,
If thou canst mutine in a matron's bones,
To flaming youth let virtue be as wax
And melt in her own fire: proclaim no shame 85
When the compulsive ardour gives the charge,
Since frost itself as actively doth burn,
And reason panders will.
*QUEEN.* O Hamlet, speak no more:
Thou turn'st mine eyes into my very soul,
And there I see such black and grained spots 90
As will not leave their tinct.
*HAM.* Nay, but to live
In the rank sweat of an enseamed bed,
Stew'd in corruption, honeying and making love

Over the nasty sty,—
*QUEEN.* O, speak to me no more;
These words like daggers enter in my ears; 95
No more, sweet Hamlet!
*HAM.* A murderer and a villain;
A slave that is not twentieth part the tithe
Of your precedent lord; a vice of kings;
A cutpurse of the empire and the rule,
That from a shelf the precious diadem stole 100
And put it in his pocket!
*QUEEN.* No more!
*HAM.* A king of shreds and patches—

*(Enter Ghost.)*

Save me, and hover o'er me with your wings,
You heavenly guards! What would your gracious
    figure?
*QUEEN.* Alas, he's mad! 105
*HAM.* Do you not come your tardy son to chide,
That, lapsed in time and passion, lets go by
The important acting of your dread command?
O, say!
*GHOST.* Do not forget: this visitation 110
Is but to whet thy almost blunted purpose.
But look, amazement on thy mother sits:
O, step between her and her fighting soul:
Conceit in weakest bodies strongest works:
Speak to her, Hamlet.
*HAM.* How is it with you, lady? 115
*QUEEN.* Alas, how is't with you,
That you do bend your eye on vacancy
And with the incorporal air do hold discourse?
Forth at your eyes your spirits wildly peep;
And, as the sleeping soldiers in the alarm, 120
Your bedded hairs, like life in excrements,
Start up and stand an end. O gentle son,
Upon the heat and flame of thy distemper
Sprinkle cool patience. Whereon do you look?
*HAM.* On him, on him! Look you, how pale he
    glares! 125
His form and cause conjoin'd, preaching to stones,

Would make them capable. Do not look upon me,
Lest with this piteous action you convert
My stern effects: then what I have to do
Will want true colour; tears perchance for blood. 130
QUEEN. To whom do you speak this?
HAM. Do you see nothing there?
QUEEN. Nothing at all; yet all that is I see.
HAM. Nor did you nothing hear?
QUEEN. No, nothing but ourselves.
HAM. Why, look you there! look, how it steals
     away!
My father, in his habit as he lived! 135
Look, where he goes, even now, out at the portal!

*(Exit Ghost.)*

QUEEN. This is the very coinage of your brain:
This bodiless creation ecstasy
Is very cunning in.
HAM. Ecstasy!
My pulse, as yours, doth temperately keep time, 140
And makes as healthful music: it is not madness
That I have utter'd: bring me to the test,
And I the matter will re-word, which madness
Would gambol from. Mother, for love of grace,
Lay not that flattering unction to your soul, 145
That not your trespass but my madness speaks:
It will but skin and film the ulcerous place,
Whiles rank corruption, mining all within,
Infects unseen. Confess yourself to heaven;
Repent what's past, avoid what is to come, 150
And do not spread the compost on the weeds,
To make them ranker. Forgive me this my virtue,
For in the fatness of these pursy times
Virtue itself of vice must pardon beg,
Yea, curb and woo for leave to do him good. 155
QUEEN. O Hamlet, thou hast cleft my heart in
     twain.
HAM. O, throw away the worser part of it,
And live the purer with the other half.
Good night: but go not to my uncle's bed;
Assume a virtue, if you have it not. 160

That monster, custom, who all sense doth eat,
Of habits devil, is angel yet in this,
That to the use of actions fair and good
He likewise gives a frock or livery,
That aptly is put on. Refrain to-night, 165
And that shall lend a kind of easiness
To the next abstinence; the next more easy;
For use almost can change the stamp of nature,
And either ... the devil, or throw him out
With wondrous potency. Once more, good
        night: 170
And when you are desirous to be blest,
I'll blessing beg of you. For this same lord,

*(Pointing to Polonius.)*

I do repent: but heaven hath pleased it so,
To punish me with this, and this with me,
That I must be their scourge and minister. 175
I will bestow him, and will answer well
The death I gave him. So, again, good night.
I must be cruel, only to be kind:
Thus bad begins, and worse remains behind.
One word more, good lady.
QUEEN. What shall I do? 180
HAM. Not this, by no means, that I bid you do:
Let the bloat king tempt you again to bed;
Pinch wanton on your cheek, call you his mouse;
And let him, for a pair of reechy kisses,
Or paddling in your neck with his damn'd fingers,

185
Make you to ravel all this matter out,
That I essentially am not in madness,
But mad in craft. 'Twere good you let him know;
For who, that's but a queen, fair, sober, wise,
Would from a paddock, from a bat, a gib, 190
Such dear concernings hide? who would do so?
No, in despite of sense and secrecy,
Unpeg the basket on the house's top,
Let the birds fly, and like the famous ape,
To try conclusions, in the basket creep 195
And break your own neck down.

QUEEN. Be thou assured, if words be made of
      breath
And breath of life, I have no life to breathe
What thou hast said to me.
HAM. I must to England; you know that?
QUEEN. Alack, 200
I had forgot: 'tis so concluded on.
HAM. There's letters seal'd: and my two
      schoolfellows,
Whom I will trust as I will adders fang'd,
They bear the mandate; they must sweep my way,
And marshal me to knavery. Let it work; 205
For 'tis the sport to have the enginer
Hoist with his own petar: and't shall go hard
But I will delve one yard below their mines,
And blow them at the moon: O, 'tis most sweet
When in one line two crafts directly meet. 210
This man shall set me packing:
I'll lug the guts into the neighbour room.
Mother, good night. Indeed this counsellor
Is now most still, most secret and most grave,
Who was in life a foolish prating knave. 215
Come, sir, to draw toward an end with you.
Good night, mother.

(*Exeunt severally; Hamlet dragging in Polonius.*)

# ACT IV

SCENE I. A ROOM IN THE CASTLE.

*(ENTER KING, QUEEN, ROSENCRANTZ, AND GUILDENSTERN.)*

> KING. There's matter in these sighs, these profound
>     heaves:
> You must translate: 'tis fit we understand them.
> Where is your son?
> QUEEN. Bestow this place on us a little while.

> *(Exeunt Rosencrantz and Guildenstern.)*

> Ah, mine own lord, what have I seen to-night! 5
> KING. What, Gertrude? How does Hamlet?
> QUEEN. Mad as the sea and wind, when both
>     contend
> Which is the mightier: in his lawless fit,
> Behind the arras hearing something stir,
> Whips out his rapier, cries 'a rat, a rat!' 10
> And in this brainish apprehension kills
> The unseen good old man.
> KING. O heavy deed!
> It had been so with us, had we been there:
> His liberty is full of threats to all,
> To you yourself, to us, to every one. 15
> Alas, how shall this bloody deed be answer'd?
> It will be laid to us, whose providence

Should have kept short, restrain'd and out of
    haunt,
This mad young man: but so much was our love,
We would not understand what was most fit, 20
But, like the owner of a foul disease,
To keep it from divulging, let it feed
Even on the pith of life. Where is he gone?
*Queen.* To draw apart the body he hath kill'd:
O'er whom his very madness, like some ore 25
Among a mineral of metals base,
Shows itself pure; he weeps for what is done.
*King.* O Gertrude, come away!
The sun no sooner shall the mountains touch,
But we will ship him hence: and this vile deed 30
We must, with all our majesty and skill,
Both countenance and excuse. Ho, Guildenstern!

(RE-ENTER ROSENCRANTZ AND GUILDENSTERN.)

Friends both, go join you with some further aid:
Hamlet in madness hath Polonius slain,
And from his mother's closet hath he dragg'd
    him: 35
Go seek him out; speak fair, and bring the body
Into the chapel. I pray you, haste in this.

(*Exeunt Rosencrantz and Guildenstern.*)

Come, Gertrude, we'll call up our wisest friends;
And let them know, both what we mean to do,
And what's untimely done.... 40
Whose whisper o'er the world's diameter
As level as the cannon to his blank
Transports his poison'd shot, may miss our name
And hit the woundless air. O, come away!
My soul is full of discord and dismay. (*Exeunt.*) 45

SCENE II. ANOTHER ROOM IN THE CASTLE

(*Enter Hamlet.*)

*Ham.* Safely stowed.

*Ros.* } *(Within)* Hamlet! Lord Hamlet!
*Guil.*}
*Ham.* But soft, what noise? who calls on Hamlet?
O, here they come.

*(Enter Rosencrantz and Guildenstern.)*

*Ros.* What have you done, my lord, with the dead
body? ₅
*Ham.* Compounded it with dust, whereto 'tis kin.
*Ros.* Tell us where 'tis, that we may take it thence
And bear it to the chapel.
*Ham.* Do not believe it.
*Ros.* Believe what? ₁₀
*Ham.* That I can keep your counsel and not mine
own. Besides, to be demanded of a sponge! what
replication
should be made by the son of a king?
*Ros.* Take you me for a sponge, my lord?
*Ham.* Ay, sir; that soaks up the king's countenance,
₁₅
his rewards, his authorities. But such officers do
the king
best service in the end: he keeps them, like an ape,
in the
corner of his jaw; first mouthed, to be last
swallowed:
when he needs what you have gleaned, it is but
squeezing
you, and, sponge, you shall be dry again. ₂₀
*Ros.* I understand you not, my lord.
*Ham.* I am glad of it: a knavish speech sleeps in a
foolish ear.
*Ros.* My lord, you must tell us where the body
is, and
go with us to the king. ₂₅
*Ham.* The body is with the king, but the king is not
with the body. The king is a thing—
*Guil.* A thing, my lord?
*Ham.* Of nothing: bring me to him. Hide fox, and
all after. *(Exeunt.)* ₃₀

## SCENE III. ANOTHER ROOM IN THE CASTLE

*(Enter King, attended.)*

KING. I have sent to seek him, and to find the body.
How dangerous is it that this man goes loose!
Yet must not we put the strong law on him:
He's loved of the distracted multitude,
Who like not in their judgement, but their eyes; 5
And where 'tis so, the offender's scourge is
    weigh'd,
But never the offence. To bear all smooth and even,
This sudden sending him away must seem
Deliberate pause: diseases desperate grown
By desperate appliance are relieved, 10
Or not at all.

*(ENTER ROSENCRANTZ.)*

How now! what hath befall'n?
ROS. Where the dead body is bestow'd, my lord,
We cannot get from him.
KING. But where is he?
ROS. Without, my lord; guarded, to know your
    pleasure.
KING. Bring him before us. 15
ROS. Ho, Guildenstern! bring in my lord.

*(ENTER HAMLET AND GUILDENSTERN.)*

KING. Now, Hamlet, where's Polonius?
HAM. At supper.
KING. At supper! where?
HAM. Not where he eats, but where he is eaten: a 20
certain convocation of politic worms are e'en at
    him. Your
worm is your only emperor for diet: we fat all
    creatures
else to fat us, and we fat ourselves for maggots:
    your fat
king and your lean beggar is but variable service,
    two

dishes, but to one table: that's the end. $_{25}$

KING. Alas, alas!

HAM. A man may fish with the worm that hath
    eat of

a king, and eat of the fish that hath fed of that
    worm.

KING. What dost thou mean by this?

HAM. Nothing but to show you how a king may go
    a $_{30}$

progress through the guts of a beggar.

KING. Where is Polonius?

HAM. In heaven; send thither to see: if your
    messenger

find him not there, seek him i' the other place
    yourself.

But indeed, if you find him not within this month,
    you $_{35}$

shall nose him as you go up the stairs into the
    lobby.

KING. Go seek him there. *(To some Attendants.)*

HAM. He will stay till you come. *(Exeunt
    Attendants.)*

KING. Hamlet, this deed, for thine especial safety,

Which we do tender, as we dearly grieve $_{40}$

For that which thou hast done, must send thee
    hence

With fiery quickness: therefore prepare thyself;

The bark is ready and the wind at help,

The associates tend, and every thing is bent

For England.

HAM. For England?

KING. Ay, Hamlet.

HAM. Good. $_{45}$

KING. So is it, if thou knew'st our purposes.

HAM. I see a cherub that sees them. But, come; for

England! Farewell, dear mother.

KING. Thy loving father, Hamlet.

HAM. My mother: father and mother is man and $_{50}$

wife; man and wife is one flesh, and so, my mother.

Come, for England! *(Exit.)*

KING. Follow him at foot; tempt him with speed
    aboard;

Delay it not; I'll have him hence to-night:
Away! for every thing is seal'd and done 55
That else leans on the affair: pray you, make haste.

*(Exeunt Rosencrantz and Guildenstern.)*

And, England, if my love thou hold'st at aught—
As my great power thereof may give thee sense,
Since yet thy cicatrice looks raw and red
After the Danish sword, and thy free awe 60
Pays homage to us—thou mayst not coldly set
Our sovereign process; which imports at full,
By letters congruing to that effect,
The present death of Hamlet. Do it, England;
For like the hectic in my blood he rages, 65
And thou must cure me: till I know 'tis done,
Howe'er my haps, my joys were ne'er begun.
    *(Exit.)*


SCENE IV. A PLAIN IN DENMARK: (ENTER
FORTINBRAS, A CAPTAIN AND SOLDIERS,
MARCHING.)

*For.* Go, captain, from me greet the Danish king;
Tell him that by his license Fortinbras
Craves the conveyance of a promised march
Over his kingdom. You know the rendezvous.
If that his majesty would aught with us, 5
We shall express our duty in his eye;
And let him know so.
*Cap.* I will do't, my lord.
*For.* Go softly on.

*(Exeunt Fortinbras and Soldiers.)*

*(Enter Hamlet, Rosencrantz, Guildenstern, and*
*others.)*

*Ham.* Good sir, whose powers are these?
*Cap.* They are of Norway, sir. 10
*Ham.* How purposed, sir, I pray you?
*Cap.* Against some part of Poland.

*HAM.* Who commands them, sir?
*CAP.* The nephew to old Norway, Fortinbras.
*HAM.* Goes it against the main of Poland, sir, 15
Or for some frontier?
*CAP.* Truly to speak, and with no addition,
We go to gain a little patch of ground
That hath in it no profit but the name.
To pay five ducats, five, I would not farm it; 20
Nor will it yield to Norway or the Pole
A ranker rate, should it be sold in fee.
*HAM.* Why, then the Polack never will defend it.
*CAP.* Yes, it is already garrison'd.
*HAM.* Two thousand souls and twenty thousand
     ducats 25
Will not debate the question of this straw:
This is the imposthume of much wealth and peace,
That inward breaks, and shows no cause without
Why the man dies. I humbly thank you, sir.
*CAP.* God be wi' you, sir. *(Exit.)*
*ROS.* Will't please you go, my lord? 30
*HAM.* I'll be with you straight. Go a little before.

*(Exeunt all but Hamlet.)*

How all occasions do inform against me,
And spur my dull revenge! What is a man,
If his chief good and market of his time
Be but to sleep and feed? a beast, no more. 35
Sure, he that made us with such large discourse,
Looking before and after, gave us not
That capability and god-like reason
To fust in us unused. Now, whether it be
Bestial oblivion, or some craven scruple 40
Of thinking too precisely on the event,—
A thought which, quarter'd, hath but one part
     wisdom
And ever three parts coward,—I do not know
Why yet I live to say 'this thing's to do,'
Sith I have cause, and will, and strength, and
     means, 45
To do't. Examples gross as earth exhort me:
Witness this army, of such mass and charge,

Led by a delicate and tender prince,
Whose spirit with divine ambition puff'd
Makes mouths at the invisible event, 50
Exposing what is mortal and unsure
To all that fortune, death and danger dare,
Even for an egg-shell. Rightly to be great
Is not to stir without great argument,
But greatly to find quarrel in a straw 55
When honour's at the stake. How stand I then,
That have a father kill'd, a mother stain'd,
Excitements of my reason and my blood,
And let all sleep, while to my shame I see
The imminent death of twenty thousand men, 60
That for a fantasy and trick of fame
Go to their graves like beds, fight for a plot
Whereon the numbers cannot try the cause,
Which is not tomb enough and continent
To hide the slain? O, from this time forth, 65
My thoughts be bloody, or be nothing worth! *(Exit.)*

## SCENE V. ELSINORE. A ROOM IN THE CASTLE.

*(Enter QUEEN, HORATIO, and a Gentleman.)*

*QUEEN.* I will not speak with her.
*GENT.* She is importunate, indeed distract:
Her mood will needs be pitied.
*QUEEN.* What would she have?
*GENT.* She speaks much of her father, says she
  hears
There's tricks i' the world, and hems and beats her
  heart, 5
Spurns enviously at straws; speaks things in doubt,
That carry but half sense: her speech is nothing,
Yet the unshaped use of it doth move
The hearers to collection; they aim at it,
And botch the words up fit to their own thoughts;
  10
Which, as her winks and nods and gestures yield
  them,
Indeed would make one think there might be
  thought,

Though nothing sure, yet much unhappily.
*Hor.* 'Twere good she were spoken with, for she
    may strew
Dangerous conjectures in ill-breeding minds. 15
*Queen.* Let her come in. *(Exit Gentleman.)*
*(Aside)* To my sick soul, as sin's true nature is,
Each toy seems prologue to some great amiss:
So full of artless jealousy is guilt,
It spills itself in fearing to be spilt. 20

*(Re-enter Gentleman, with Ophelia.)*

*Oph.* Where is the beauteous majesty of Denmark?
*Queen.* How now, Ophelia!
*Oph. (Sings)* How should I your true love know
From another one?
By his cockle hat and staff 25
And his sandal shoon.
*Queen.* Alas, sweet lady, what imports this song?
*Oph.* Say you? nay, pray you, mark.
*(Sings)* He is dead and gone, lady,
He is dead and gone; 30
At his head a grass-green turf,
At his heels a stone.
Oh, oh!
*Queen.* Nay, but, Ophelia,—
*Oph.* Pray you, mark.
*(Sings)* White his shroud as the mountain snow,—

*(Enter King.)*

*Queen.* Alas, look here, my lord. 35
*Oph. (Sings)* Larded with sweet flowers;
Which bewept to the grave did go
With true-love showers.
*King.* How do you, pretty lady?
*Oph.* Well, God 'ild you! They say the owl was
    a 40
baker's daughter. Lord, we know what we are,
    but know
not what we may be. God be at your table!
*King.* Conceit upon her father.

*Oph.* Pray you, let's have no words of this;
    but when
they ask you what it means, say you this: 45
*(Sings)* To-morrow is Saint Valentine's day,
All in the morning betime,
And I a maid at your window,
To be your Valentine.
Then up he rose, and donn'd his clothes, 50
And dupp'd the chamber-door;
Let in the maid, that out a maid
Never departed more.
*King.* Pretty Ophelia!
*Oph.* Indeed, la, without an oath, I'll make an end
    on't: 55
*(Sings)* By Gis and by Saint Charity,
Alack, and fie for shame!
Young men will do't, if they come to't;
By cock, they are to blame.
Quoth she, before you tumbled me, 60
You promised me to wed.
He answers:
So would I ha' done, by yonder sun,
An thou hadst not come to my bed.
*King.* How long hath she been thus?
*Oph.* I hope all will be well. We must be patient:
    but 65
I cannot choose but weep, to think they should lay
    him i'
the cold ground. My brother shall know of it: and
    so I
thank you for your good counsel. Come, my coach!
Good night, ladies; good night, sweet ladies; good
    night,
good night. *(Exit.)* 70
*King.* Follow her close; give her good watch, I pray
    you. *(Exit Horatio.)*
O, this is the poison of deep grief; it springs
All from her father's death. O Gertrude, Gertrude,
When sorrows come, they come not single spies,
But in battalions! First, her father slain: 75
Next, your son gone; and he most violent author
Of his own just remove: the people muddied,

Thick and unwholesome in their thoughts and
    whispers,
For good Polonius' death; and we have done but
    greenly,
In hugger-mugger to inter him: poor Ophelia 80
Divided from herself and her fair judgement,
Without the which we are pictures, or mere beasts:
Last, and as much containing as all these,
Her brother is in secret come from France,
Feeds on his wonder, keeps himself in clouds, 85
And wants not buzzers to infect his ear
With pestilent speeches of his father's death;
Wherein necessity, of matter beggar'd,
Will nothing stick our person to arraign
In ear and ear. O my dear Gertrude, this, 90
Like to a murdering-piece, in many places
Gives me superfluous death. *(A noise within.)*
QUEEN. Alack, what noise is this?
KING. Where are my Switzers? Let them guard the
    door.

*(Enter another Gentleman.)*

What is the matter?
GENT. Save yourself, my lord:
The ocean, overpeering of his list, 95
Eats not the flats with more impetuous haste
Than young Laertes, in a riotous head,
O'erbears your officers. The rabble call him lord;
And, as the world were now but to begin,
Antiquity forgot, custom not known, 100
The ratifiers and props of every word,
They cry 'Choose we; Laertes shall be king!'
Caps, hands and tongues applaud it to the clouds,
'Laertes shall be king, Laertes king!'
QUEEN. How cheerfully on the false trail they
    cry! 105
O, this is counter, you false Danish dogs! *(Noise
    within.)*
KING. The doors are broke.

*(Enter LAERTES, armed; Danes following.)*

*LAER.* Where is this king? Sirs, stand you all
 without.
*DANES.* No, let's come in.
*LAER.* I pray you, give me leave.
*DANES.* We will, we will. 110

*(They retire without the door.)*

*LAER.* I thank you: keep the door. O thou vile king,
Give me my father!
*QUEEN.* Calmly, good Laertes.
*LAER.* That drop of blood that's calm proclaims me
 bastard;
Cries cuckold to my father; brands the harlot
Even here, between the chaste unsmirched brow 115
Of my true mother.
*KING.* What is the cause, Laertes,
That thy rebellion looks so giant-like?
Let him go, Gertrude; do not fear our person:
There's such divinity doth hedge a king,
That treason can but peep to what it would, 120
Acts little of his will. Tell me, Laertes,
Why thou art thus incensed: let him go, Gertrude:
Speak, man.
*LAER.* Where is my father?
*KING.* Dead.
*QUEEN.* But not by him.
*KING.* Let him demand his fill. 125
*LAER.* How came he dead? I'll not be juggled
 with:
To hell, allegiance! vows, to the blackest devil!
Conscience and grace, to the profoundest pit!
I dare damnation: to this point I stand,
That both the worlds I give to negligence, 130
Let come what comes; only I'll be revenged
Most throughly for my father.
*KING.* Who shall stay you?
*LAER.* My will, not all the world:
And for my means, I'll husband them so well,
They shall go far with little.
*KING.* Good Laertes, 135
If you desire to know the certainty

Of your dear father's death, is't writ in your
    revenge,
That, swoopstake, you will draw both friend
    and foe,
Winner and loser?
*LAER.* None but his enemies.
*KING.* Will you know them then? 140
*LAER.* To his good friends thus wide I'll ope my
    arms;
And, like the kind life-rendering pelican,
Repast them with my blood.
*KING.*         Why, now you speak
Like a good child and a true gentleman.
That I am guiltless of your father's death, 145
And am most sensibly in grief for it,
It shall as level to your judgement pierce
As day does to your eye.
*DANES. (Within)* Let her come in.
*LAER.* How now! what noise is that?

*(Re-enter OPHELIA.)*

O heat, dry up my brains! tears seven times salt, 150
Burn out the sense and virtue of mine eye!
By heaven, thy madness shall be paid with weight,
Till our scale turn the beam. O rose of May!
Dear maid, kind sister, sweet Ophelia!
O heavens! is't possible a young maid's wits 155
Should be as mortal as an old man's life?
Nature is fine in love, and where 'tis fine
It sends some precious instance of itself
After the thing it loves.
*OPH. (Sings)* They bore him barefaced on the
    bier; 160
Hey non nonny, nonny, hey nonny:
And in his grave rain'd many a tear,—
Fare you well, my dove!
*LAER.* Hadst thou thy wits, and didst persuade
    revenge,
It could not move thus. 165
*OPH. (Sings)* You must sing down a-down,
An you call him a-down-a.

O, how the wheel becomes it! It is the false stew-
    ard, that
stole his master's daughter.
*LAER.* This nothing's more than matter. 170
*OPH.* There's rosemary, that's for remembrance:
    pray
you, love, remember: and there is pansies, that's for
thoughts.
*LAER.* A document in madness; thoughts and re-
    membrance
fitted. 175
*OPH.* There's fennel for you, and columbines:
    there's
rue for you; and here's some for me: we may call
    it herb
of grace o' Sundays: O, you must wear your rue
    with a
difference. There's a daisy: I would give you some
violets, but they withered all when my father died:
    they 180
say a' made a good end,—
*(Sings)* For bonny sweet Robin is all my joy.
*LAER.* Thought and affliction, passion, hell itself,
She turns to favour and to prettiness.
*OPH. (Sings)* And will a' not come again? 185
And will a' not come again?
No, no, he is dead,
Go to thy death-bed,
He never will come again.
His beard was as white as snow, 190
All flaxen was his poll:
He is gone, he is gone,
And we cast away moan:
God ha' mercy on his soul!
And of all Christian souls, I pray God. God be wi'
    you. 195

                                        *(Exit.)*


*LAER.* Do you see this, O God?
*KING.* Laertes, I must commune with your grief,
Or you deny me right. Go but apart,

Make choice of whom your wisest friends you will,
And they shall hear and judge 'twixt you and
     me: 200
If by direct or by collateral hand
They find us touch'd, we will our kingdom give,
Our crown, our life, and all that we call ours,
To you in satisfaction; but if not,
Be you content to lend your patience to us, 205
And we shall jointly labour with your soul
To give it due content.
*LAER.* Let this be so;
His means of death, his obscure funeral,
No trophy, sword, nor hatchment o'er his bones,
No noble rite nor formal ostentation, 210
Cry to be heard, as 'twere from heaven to earth,
That I must call't in question.
*KING.* So you shall;
And where the offence is let the great axe fall.
I pray you, go with me. *(Exeunt.)*

SCENE VI. ANOTHER ROOM IN THE CASTLE:
(ENTER HORATIO AND A SERVANT.)

*HOR.* What are they that would speak with me?
*SERV.* Sea-faring men, sir: they say they have letters
     for you.
*HOR.* Let them come in. *(Exit Servant.)*
I do not know from what part of the world
I should be greeted, if not from Lord Hamlet. 5

*(Enter Sailors.)*

*FIRST SAIL.* God bless you, sir.
*HOR.* Let him bless thee too.
*FIRST SAIL.* He shall, sir, an't please him. There's a
letter for you, sir; it comes from the ambassador
     that was
bound for England; if your name be Horatio, as I
     am let 10
to know it is.
*HOR.* *(Read)* 'Horatio, when thou shalt have over-
     looked

this, give these fellows some means to the king:
they have letters for him. Ere we were two days old at
sea, a pirate of very warlike appointment gave us chase. 15
Finding ourselves too slow of sail, we put on a compelled
valour: and in the grapple I boarded them: on the instant
they got clear of our ship; so I alone became their prisoner.
They have dealt with me like thieves of mercy:
but they knew what they did; I am to do a good turn 20
for them. Let the king have the letters I have sent; and
repair thou to me with as much speed as thou wouldest
fly death. I have words to speak in thine ear will make
thee dumb; yet are they much too light for the bore of
the matter. These good fellows will bring thee where I 25
am. Rosencrantz and Guildenstern hold their course for
England: of them I have much to tell thee. Farewell.
'He that thou knowest thine, Hamlet.'
Come, I will make you way for these your letters;
And do't the speedier, that you may direct me 30
To him from whom you brought them. *(Exeunt.)*


SCENE VII. ANOTHER ROOM IN THE CASTLE:
(ENTER KING AND LAERTES.)

*KING.* Now must your conscience my acquittance seal,
And you must put me in your heart for friend,
Sith you have heard, and with a knowing ear,
That he which hath your noble father slain
Pursued my life.
*LAER.* It well appears: but tell me 5

Why you proceeded not against these feats,
So crimeful and so capital in nature,
As by your safety, wisdom, all things else,
You mainly were stirr'd up.
*KING.* O, for two special reasons,
Which may to you perhaps seem much unsinew'd,
But yet to me they're strong. The queen his mother 10
Lives almost by his looks; and for myself—
My virtue or my plague, be it either which—
She's so conjunctive to my life and soul,
That, as the star moves not but in his sphere, 15
I could not but by her. The other motive,
Why to a public count I might not go,
Is the great love the general gender bear him;
Who, dipping all his faults in their affection,
Would, like the spring that turneth wood to
      stone, 20
Convert his gyves to graces; so that my arrows,
Too slightly timber'd for so loud a wind,
Would have reverted to my bow again
And not where I had aim'd them.
*LAER.* And so have I a noble father lost; 25
A sister driven into desperate terms,
Whose worth, if praises may go back again,
Stood challenger on mount of all the age
For her perfections: but my revenge will come.
*KING.* Break not your sleeps for that: you must not
      think 30
That we are made of stuff so flat and dull
That we can let our beard be shook with danger
And think it pastime. You shortly shall hear more:
I loved your father, and we love ourself;
And that, I hope, will teach you to imagine— 35

*(Enter a Messenger, with letters.)*

How now! what news?
*MESS.* Letters, my lord, from Hamlet:
This to your majesty; this to the queen.
*KING.* From Hamlet! who brought them?
*MESS.* Sailors, my lord, they say; I saw them not:

They were given me by Claudio; he received
    them 40
Of him that brought them.
*KING.* Laertes, you shall hear them.
*Leave us. (Exit Messenger.)*
*(Read)* 'High and mighty, You shall know I am set
naked on your kingdom. To-morrow shall I beg
    leave
to see your kingly eyes: when I shall, first asking
    your 45
pardon thereunto, recount the occasion of my
    sudden and
more strange return.
'Hamlet.'
What should this mean? Are all the rest come back?
Or is it some abuse, and no such thing? 50
*LAER.* Know you the hand?
*KING.* 'Tis Hamlet's character. 'Naked!'
And in a postscript here, he says 'alone.'
Can you advise me?
*LAER.* I'm lost in it, my lord. But let him come; 55
It warms the very sickness in my heart,
That I shall live and tell him to his teeth,
'Thus didest thou.'
*KING.* If it be so, Laertes,—
As how should it be so? how otherwise?—
Will you be ruled by me?
*LAER.* Ay, my lord; 60
So you will not o'errule me to a peace.
*KING.* To thine own peace. If he be now return'd,
As checking at his voyage, and that he means
No more to undertake it, I will work him
To an exploit now ripe in my device, 65
Under the which he shall not choose but fall:
And for his death no wind of blame shall breathe;
But even his mother shall uncharge the practice,
And call it accident.
*LAER.* My lord, I will be ruled;
The rather, if you could devise it so 70
That I might be the organ.
*KING.* It falls right.
You have been talk'd of since your travel much,

And that in Hamlet's hearing, for a quality
Wherein, they say, you shine: your sum of parts
Did not together pluck such envy from him, 75
As did that one, and that in my regard
Of the unworthiest siege.
*LAER.* What part is that, my lord?
*KING.* A very riband in the cap of youth,
Yet needful too; for youth no less becomes
The light and careless livery that it wears 80
Than settled age his sables and his weeds,
Importing health and graveness. Two months
    since,
Here was a gentleman of Normandy:—
I've seen myself, and served against, the French,
And they can well on horseback: but this gallant 85
Had witchcraft in't; he grew unto his seat,
And to such wondrous doing brought his horse
As had he been incorpsed and demi-natured
With the brave beast: so far he topp'd my thought
That I, in forgery of shapes and tricks, 90
Come short of what he did.
*LAER.* A Norman was't?
*KING.* A Norman.
*LAER.* Upon my life, Lamond.
*KING.* The very same.
*LAER.* I know him well: he is the brooch indeed
And gem of all the nation. 95
*KING.* He made confession of you,
And gave you such a masterly report,
For art and exercise in your defence,
And for your rapier most especial,
That he cried out, 'twould be a sight indeed 100
If one could match you: the scrimers of their
    nation.
He swore, had neither motion, guard, nor eye,
If you opposed them. Sir, this report of his
Did Hamlet so envenom with his envy
That he could nothing do but wish and beg 105
Your sudden coming o'er, to play with him.
Now, out of this—
*LAER.* What out of this, my lord?
*KING.* Laertes, was your father dear to you?

Or are you like the painting of a sorrow,
A face without a heart?
LAER. Why ask you this? 110
KING. Not that I think you did not love your father,
But that I know love is begun by time,
And that I see, in passages of proof,
Time qualifies the spark and fire of it.
There lives within the very flame of love 115
A kind of wick or snuff that will abate it;
And nothing is at a like goodness still,
For goodness, growing to a plurisy,
Dies in his own too much: that we would do
We should do when we would; for this 'would'
        changes 120
And hath abatements and delays as many
As there are tongues, are hands, are accidents,
And then this 'should' is like a spendthrift sigh,
That hurts by easing. But, to the quick o' the ulcer:
Hamlet comes back: what would you undertake,

125
To show yourself your father's son in deed
More than in words?
LAER. To cut his throat i' the church.
KING. No place indeed should murder sanctuarize;
Revenge should have no bounds. But, good
        Laertes,
Will you do this, keep close within your chamBER.

130
Hamlet return'd shall know you are come home:
We'll put on those shall praise your excellence
And set a double varnish on the fame
The Frenchman gave you; bring you in fine
        together
And wager on your heads: he, being remiss, 135
Most generous and free from all contriving,
Will not peruse the foils, so that with ease,
Or with a little shuffling, you may choose
A sword unbated, and in a pass of practice
Requite him for your father.
LAER. I will do't 140
And for that purpose I'll anoint my sword.
I bought an unction of a mountebank,

So mortal that but dip a knife in it,
Where it draws blood no cataplasm so rare,
Collected from all simples that have virtue $_{145}$
Under the moon, can save the thing from death
That is but scratch'd withal: I'll touch my point
With this contagion, that, if I gall him slightly,
It may be death.
*KING.* Let's further think of this;
Weigh what convenience both of time and
    means $_{150}$
May fit us to our shape: if this should fail,
And that our drift look through our bad per-
    formance,
'Twere better not assay'd: therefore this project
Should have a back or second, that might hold
If this did blast in proof. Soft! let me see: $_{155}$
We'll make a solemn wager on your cunnings:
I ha't:
When in your motion you are hot and dry—
As make your bouts more violent to that end—
And that he calls for drink, I'll have prepared
    him $_{160}$
A chalice for the nonce; whereon but sipping,
If he by chance escape your venom'd stuck,
Our purpose may hold there. But stay, what noise?

*(Enter QUEEN.)*

How now, sweet queen!
*QUEEN.* One woe doth tread upon another's
    heel, $_{165}$
So fast they follow: your sister's drown'd, Laertes.
*LAER.* Drown'd! O, where?
*QUEEN.* There is a willow grows aslant a brook,
That shows his hoar leaves in the glassy stream;
There with fantastic garlands did she come $_{170}$
Of crow-flowers, nettles, daisies, and long purples,
That liberal shepherds give a grosser name,
But our cold maids do dead men's fingers call
    them:
There, on the pendent boughs her coronet weeds
Clambering to hang, an envious sliver broke; $_{175}$

When down her weedy trophies and herself
Fell in the weeping brook. Her clothes spread wide,
And mermaid-like awhile they bore her up:
Which time she chanted snatches of old tunes,
As one incapable of her own distress, 180
Or like a creature native and indued
Unto that element: but long it could not be
Till that her garments, heavy with their drink,
Pull'd the poor wretch from her melodious lay
To muddy death.
*LAER.* Alas, then she is drown'd! 185
*QUEEN.* Drown'd, drown'd.
*LAER.* Too much of water hast thou, poor Ophelia,
And therefore I forbid my tears: but yet
It is our trick; nature her custom holds,
Let shame say what it will: when these are gone, 190
The woman will be out. Adieu, my lord:
I have a speech of fire that fain would blaze,
But that this folly douts it. *(Exit.)*
*KING.* Let's follow, Gertrude:
How much I had to do to calm his rage!
Now fear I this will give it start again; 195
Therefore let's follow. *(Exeunt.)*

# ACT V

SCENE I. A CHURCHYARD.

*(Enter two Clowns, with spades, &c.)*

*First Clo.* Is she to be buried in Christian burial that
willfully seeks her own salvation?
*Sec. Clo.* I tell thee she is; and therefore make her
grave straight: the crowner hath sat on her, and finds it
Christian burial. ₅
*First Clo.* How can that be, unless she drowned herself
in her own defence?
*Sec. Clo.* Why, 'tis found so.
*First Clo.* It must be 'se offendendo;' it cannot be else.
For here lies the point: if I drown myself wittingly, it argues ₁₀
an act: and an act hath three branches; it is, to act, to
do, and to perform: argal, she drowned herself wittingly.
*Sec. Clo.* Nay, but hear you, goodman delver.
*First Clo.* Give me leave. Here lies the water; good:

here stands the man; good: if the man go to this
water and $_{15}$

drown himself, it is, will he, nill he, he goes;
mark you

that; but if the water come to him and drown
him, he

drowns not himself: argal, he that is not guilty of
his own

death shortens not his own life.

*Sec. Clo.* But is this law? $_{20}$

*First Clo.* Ay, marry, is't; crowner's quest law.

*Sec. Clo.* Will you ha' the truth on't? If this
had not

been a gentlewoman, she should have been buried
out o'

Christian burial.

*First Clo.* Why, there thou say'st: and the more
pity that $_{25}$

great folk should have countenance in this world to
drown

or hang themselves, more than their even Christian. Come,

my spade. There is no ancient gentlemen but
gardeners,

ditchers and grave-makers: they hold up Adam's
profession.

*Sec. Clo.* Was he a gentleman? $_{30}$

*First Clo.* A' was the first that ever bore arms.

*Sec. Clo.* Why, he had none.

*First Clo.* What, art a heathen? How dost thou
understand

the Scripture? The Scripture says Adam digged:
could he dig without arms? I'll put another question $_{35}$

to thee: if thou answerest me not to the purpose,
confess

thyself—

*Sec. Clo.* Go to.

*First Clo.* What is he that builds stronger than
either

the mason, the shipwright, or the carpenter? $_{40}$

*Sec. Clo.* The gallows-maker; for that frame out-
lives a
thousand tenants.
*First Clo.* I like thy wit well, in good faith: the
gallows
does well; but how does it well? it does well to
those that
do ill: now, thou dost ill to say the gallows is built
stronger 45
than the church: argal, the gallows may do well to
thee.
To't again, come.
*Sec. Clo.* 'Who builds stronger than a mason, a
shipwright,
or a carpenter?'
*First Clo.* Ay, tell me that, and unyoke. 50
*Sec. Clo.* Marry, now I can tell.
*First Clo.* To't.
*Sec. Clo.* Mass, I cannot tell.

*(Enter HAMLET and HORATIO, afar off.)*

*First Clo.* Cudgel thy brains no more about it,
for your
dull ass will not mend his pace with beating, and
when 55
you are asked this question next, say 'a
grave-maker:' the
houses that he makes last till doomsday. Go, get
thee to
Yaughan; fetch me a stoup of liquor. *(Exit Sec.
Clown.)*

*(He digs, and sings.)*

In youth, when I did love, did love,
Methought it was very sweet, 60
To contract, O, the time, for-a my behove,
O, methought, there-a was nothing-a meet.
*Ham.* Has this fellow no feeling of his business, that
he sings at grave-making?

*Hor.* Custom hath made it in him a property of
easiness. 65

*Ham.* 'Tis e'en so: the hand of little employment
hath

the daintier sense.

*First Clo. (Sing)* But age, with his stealing steps,
Hath claw'd me in his clutch, 70
And hath shipped me intil the land,
As if I had never been such.

*(Throws up a skull.)*

*Ham.* That skull had a tongue in it, and could sing
once: how the knave jowls it to the ground, as if
it were

Cain's jaw-bone, that did the first murder! It might
be 75

the pate of a politician, which this ass now o'er-
reaches;

one that would circumvent God, might it not?

*Hor.* It might, my lord.

*Ham.* Or of a courtier, which could say 'Good
morrow,

sweet lord! How dost thou, sweet lord?' This
might 80

be my lord such-a-one, that praised my lord such-
a-one's

horse, when he meant to beg it; might it not?

*Hor.* Ay, my lord.

*Ham.* Why, e'en so: and now my Lady Worm's;
chapless, and knocked about the mazzard with a
sexton's 85

spade: here's fine revolution, an we had the trick to
see't.

Did these bones cost no more the breeding, but to
play at

loggats with 'em? mine ache to think on't.

*First Clo. (Sing)* A pick-axe, and a spade, a spade,
For and a shrouding sheet: 90
O, a pit of clay for to be made
For such a guest is meet.

*(Throws up another skull.)*

*Ham.* There's another: why may not that be the
  skull

of a lawyer? Where be his quiddities now, his quil-
  lets, his

cases, his tenures, and his tricks? why does he
  suffer this ₉₅

rude knave now to knock him about the sconce
  with a dirty

shovel, and will not tell him of his action of bat-
  tery? Hum!

This fellow might be in 's time a great buyer of
  land, with

his statutes, his recognizances, his fines, his double
  vouchers,

his recoveries: is this the fine of his fines and the
  recovery ₁₀₀

of his recoveries, to have his fine pate full of fine
  dirt? will

his vouchers vouch him no more of his purchases,
  and double

ones too, than the length and breadth of a pair of
  indentures?

The very conveyances of his lands will hardly lie in

this box; and must the inheritor himself have no
  more, ha? ₁₀₅

*Hor.* Not a jot more, my lord.

*Ham.* Is not parchment made of sheep-skins?

*Hor.* Ay, my lord, and of calf-skins too.

*Ham.* They are sheep and calves which seek out
  assurance

in that. I will speak to this fellow. Whose grave's ₁₁₀
this, sirrah?

*First Clo.* Mine, sir.

*(Sing)* O, a pit of clay for to be made

For such a guest is meet.

*Ham.* I think it be thine indeed, for thou liest
  in't. ₁₁₅

*First Clo.* You lie out on't, sir, and therefore
  'tis not

yours: for my part, I do not lie in't, and yet it is
    mine.

*Ham.* Thou dost lie in't, to be in't and say it is thine:
'tis for the dead, not for the quick; therefore thou
    liest.

*First Clo.* 'Tis a quick lie, sir; 'twill away again,
    from 120
me to you.

*Ham.* What man dost thou dig it for?

*First Clo.* For no man, sir.

*Ham.* What woman then?

*First Clo.* For none, neither. 125

*Ham.* Who is to be buried in 't?

*First Clo.* One that was a woman, sir; but, rest her
soul, she's dead.

*Ham.* How absolute the knave is! we must speak by
the card, or equivocation will undo us. By the
    Lord, 130
Horatio, this three years I have taken note of it;
    the age
is grown so picked that the toe of the peasant
    comes so
near the heel of the courtier, he galls his kibe.
    How long
hast thou been a grave-maker?

*First Clo.* Of all the days i' the year, I came to't
    that 135
day that our last king Hamlet o'ercame Fortinbras.

*Ham.* How long is that since?

*First Clo.* Cannot you tell that? every fool can tell
that: it was that very day that young Hamlet was
    born;
he that is mad, and sent into England. 140

*Ham.* Ay, marry, why was he sent into England?

*First Clo.* Why, because a' was mad: a' shall
    recover
his wits there; or, if a' do not, 'tis no great matter
    there.

*Ham.* Why?

*First Clo.* 'Twill not be seen in him there; there
    the 145
men are as mad as he.

*Ham.* How came he mad?

*First Clo.* Very strangely, they say.

*Ham.* How 'strangely'?

*First Clo.* Faith, e'en with losing his wits. 150

*Ham.* Upon what ground?

*First Clo.* Why, here in Denmark: I have been sexton

here, man and boy, thirty years.

*Ham.* How long will a man lie i' the earth ere he rot?

*First Clo.* I'faith, if a' be not rotten before a' die —as 155

we have many pocky corses now-a-days, that will scarce

hold the laying in—a' will last you some eight year or nine

year: a tanner will last you nine year.

*Ham.* Why he more than another?

*First Clo.* Why, sir, his hide is so tanned with his trade 160

that a' will keep out water a great while; and your water is

a sore decayer of your whoreson dead body. Here's a skull

now: this skull has lain in the earth three and twenty years.

*Ham.* Whose was it?

*First Clo.* A whoreson mad fellow's it was: whose do 165

you think it was?

*Ham.* Nay, I know not.

*First Clo.* A pestilence on him for a mad rogue! a' poured a flagon of Rhenish on my head once. This same

skull, sir, was Yorick's skull, the king's jester. 170

*Ham.* This?

*First Clo.* E'en that.

*Ham.* Let me see. *(Takes the skull.)* Alas, poor Yorick! I knew him, Horatio: a fellow of infinite jest, of

most excellent fancy: he hath borne me on his back a 175

thousand times; and now how abhorred in my
    imagination
it is! my gorge rises at it. Here hung those lips that I
have kissed I know not how oft. Where be your
    gibes
now? your gambols? your songs? your flashes of
    merriment,
that were wont to set the table on a roar? Not
    one 180
now, to mock your own grinning? quite
    chop-fallen? Now
get you to my lady's chamber, and tell her, let her
    paint
an inch thick, to this favour she must come;
    make her
laugh at that. Prithee, Horatio, tell me one thing.
*Hor.* What's that, my lord? 185
*Ham.* Dost thou think Alexander looked o' this
    fashion
i' the earth?
*Hor.* E'en so.
*Ham. And smelt so? pah! (Puts down the skull.)*
*Hor.* E'en so, my lord. 190
*Ham.* To what base uses we may return, Horatio!
Why may not imagination trace the noble dust of
    Alexander,
till he find it stopping a bung-hole?
*Hor.* 'Twere to consider too curiously, to consider
    so.
*Ham.* No, faith, not a jot; but to follow him
    thither 195
with modesty enough and likelihood to lead it: as
    thus:
Alexander died, Alexander was buried, Alexander
    returneth
into dust; the dust is earth; of earth we make loam;
and why of that loam, whereto he was converted,
    might
they not stop a beer-barrel? 200
Imperious Cæsar, dead and turn'd to clay,
Might stop a hole to keep the wind away:
O, that that earth, which kept the world in awe,

Should patch a wall to expel the winter's flaw!
But soft! but soft! aside: here comes the king. 205

*(Enter Priests, &c. in procession; the Corpse of Ophelia,
LAERTES and Mourners following; KING, QUEEN, their trains,
&c.)*

The queen, the courtiers: who is this they follow?
And with such maimed rites? This doth betoken
The corse they follow did with desperate hand
Fordo its own life: 'twas of some estate.
Couch we awhile, and mark. *(Retiring with Horatio.)*

210
*LAER.* What ceremony else?
*HAM.* That is Laertes, a very noble youth: mark.
*LAER.* What ceremony else?
*FIRST PRIEST.* Her obsequies have been as far
    enlarged
As we have warranty: her death was doubtful; 215
And, but that great command o'ersways the order,
She should in ground unsanctified have lodged
Till the last trumpet; for charitable prayers,
Shards, flints and pebbles should be thrown
    on her:
Yet here she is allow'd her virgin crants, 220
Her maiden strewments and the bringing home
Of bell and burial.
*LAER.* Must there no more be done?
*FIRST PRIEST.* No more be done:
We should profane the service of the dead
To sing a requiem and such rest to her 225
As to peace-parted souls.
*LAER.* Lay her i' the earth:
And from her fair and unpolluted flesh
May violets spring! I tell thee, churlish priest,
A ministering angel shall my sister be,
When thou liest howling.
*HAM.* What, the fair Ophelia! 230
*QUEEN.* *(Scattering flower)* Sweets to the sweet:
    farewell!
I hoped thou shouldst have been my Hamlet's
    wife;

I thought thy bride-bed to have deck'd, sweet
   maid,
And not have strew'd thy grave.
*LAER.* O, treble woe
Fall ten times treble on that cursed head <sub>235</sub>
Whose wicked deed thy most ingenious sense
Deprived thee of! Hold off the earth awhile,
Till I have caught her once more in mine arms:

*(Leaps into the grave.)*

Now pile your dust upon the quick and dead,
Till of this flat a mountain you have made <sub>240</sub>
To o'ertop old Pelion or the skyish head
Of blue Olympus.
*HAM. (Advancing)* What is he whose grief
Bears such an emphasis? whose phrase of sorrow
Conjures the wandering stars and makes them
   stand
Like wonder-wounded hearers? This is I, <sub>245</sub>
*Hamlet the Dane. (Leaps into the grave.)*
*LAER.* The devil take thy soul!

*(Grappling with him.)*

*HAM.* Thou pray'st not well.
I prithee, take thy fingers from my throat;
For, though I am not splenitive and rash,
Yet have I in me something dangerous, <sub>250</sub>
Which let thy wisdom fear. Hold off thy hand.
*KING.* Pluck them asunder.
*QUEEN.* Hamlet, Hamlet!
*ALL.* Gentlemen,—
*HOR.* Good my lord, be quiet.

*(The Attendants part them, and they come out of the grave.)*

*HAM.* Why, I will fight with him upon this theme
Until my eyelids will no longer wag. <sub>255</sub>
*QUEEN.* O my son, what theme?
*HAM.* I loved Ophelia: forty thousand brothers
Could not, with all their quantity of love,

Make up my sum. What wilt thou do for her?
KING. O, he is mad, Laertes. 260
QUEEN. For love of God, forbear him.
HAM. 'Swounds, show me what thou'lt do:
Woo't weep? woo't fight? woo't fast? woo't tear
    thyself?
Woo't drink up eisel? eat a crocodile?
I'll do't. Dost thou come here to whine? 265
To outface me with leaping in her grave?
Be buried quick with her, and so will I:
And, if thou prate of mountains, let them throw
Millions of acres on us, till our ground,
Singeing his pate against the burning zone, 270
Make Ossa like a wart! Nay, an thou'lt mouth,
I'll rant as well as thou.
QUEEN. This is mere madness:
And thus awhile the fit will work on him;
Anon, as patient as the female dove
When that her golden couplets are disclosed, 275
His silence will sit drooping.
HAM. Hear you, sir;
What is the reason that you use me thus?
I loved you ever: but it is no matter;
Let Hercules himself do what he may,
The cat will mew, and dog will have his day.
    (Exit.) 280
King. I pray thee, good Horatio, wait upon him.

(Exit Horatio.)


(To Laertes) Strengthen your patience in our last
    night's speech;
We'll put the matter to the present push.
Good Gertrude, set some watch over your son.
This grave shall have a living monument: 285
An hour of quiet shortly shall we see;
Till then, in patience our proceeding be. (Exeunt.)


SCENE II. A HALL IN THE CASTLE

(Enter Hamlet and Horatio.)

*Ham.* So much for this, sir: now shall you see the
    other;
You do remember all the circumstance?
*Hor.* Remember it, my lord!
*Ham.* Sir, in my heart there was a kind of fighting,
That would not let me sleep: methought I lay 5
Worse than the mutines in the bilboes. Rashly,
And praised be rashness for it, let us know,
Our indiscretion sometime serves us well
When our deep plots do pall; and that should
    learn us
There's a divinity that shapes our ends, 10
Rough-hew them how we will.
*Hor.* That is most certain.
*Ham.* Up from my cabin,
My sea-gown scarf'd about me, in the dark
Groped I to find out them; had my desire,
Finger'd their packet, and in fine withdrew 15
To mine own room again; making so bold,
My fears forgetting manners, to unseal
Their grand commission; where I found, Horatio,—
O royal knavery!—an exact command,
Larded with many several sorts of reasons, 20
Importing Denmark's health and England's too,
With, ho! such bugs and goblins in my life,
That, on the supervise, no leisure bated,
No, not to stay the grinding of the axe,
My head should be struck off.
*Hor.* Is't possible? 25
*Ham.* Here's the commission: read it at more
    leisure.
But wilt thou hear now how I did proceed?
*Hor.* I beseech you.
*Ham.* Being thus be-netted round with villanies,—
Or I could make a prologue to my brains, 30
They had begun the play,—I sat me down;
Devised a new commission; wrote it fair:
I once did hold it, as our statists do,
A baseness to write fair, and labour'd much
How to forget that learning; but, sir, now 35
It did me yeoman's service: wilt thou know
The effect of what I wrote?

*Hor.* Ay, good my lord.
*Ham.* An earnest conjuration from the king,
As England was his faithful tributary,
As love between them like the palm might flourish,

40
As peace should still her wheaten garland wear
And stand a comma 'tween their amities,
And many such-like 'As'es of great charge,
That, on the view and knowing of these contents,
Without debatement further, more or less, 45
He should the bearers put to sudden death,
Not shriving-time allow'd.
*Hor.* How was this seal'd?
*Ham.* Why, even in that was heaven ordinant.
I had my father's signet in my purse,
Which was the model of that Danish seal: 50
Folded the writ up in the form of the other;
Subscribed it; gave't the impression; placed it
    safely,
The changeling never known. Now, the next day
Was our sea-fight; and what to this was sequent
Thou know'st already. 55
*Hor.* So Guildenstern and Rosencrantz go to't.
*Ham.* Why, man, they did make love to this em-
    ployment;
They are not near my conscience; their defeat
Does by their own insinuation grow:
'Tis dangerous when the baser nature comes 60
Between the pass and fell incensed points
Of mighty opposites.
*Hor.* Why, what a king is this!
*Ham.* Does it not, thinks't thee, stand me now
    upon—
He that hath kill'd my king, and whored my
    mother;
Popp'd in between the election and my hopes; 65
Thrown out his angle for my proper life,
And with such cozenage—is't not perfect con-
    science,
To quit him with this arm? and is't not to be
    damn'd,
To let this canker of our nature come

In further evil? 70
Hor. It must be shortly known to him from
    England
What is the issue of the business there.
Ham. It will be short: the interim is mine;
And a man's life's no more than to say 'One.'
But I am very sorry, good Horatio, 75
That to Laertes I forgot myself;
For, by the image of my cause, I see
The portraiture of his: I'll court his favours:
But, sure, the bravery of his grief did put me
Into a towering passion.
Hor. Peace! who comes here? 80

*(Enter Osric.)*

Osr. Your lordship is right welcome back to
    Denmark.
Ham. I humbly thank you, sir. Dost know this
    water-fly?
Hor. No, my good lord.
Ham. Thy state is the more gracious, for 'tis a
    vice to
know him. He hath much land, and fertile: let a
    beast be 85
lord of beasts, and his crib shall stand at the king's
    mess:
'tis a chough, but, as I say, spacious in the posses-
    sion of dirt.
Osr. Sweet lord, if your lordship were at leisure, I
should impart a thing to you from his majesty.
Ham. I will receive it, sir, with all diligence of
    spirit. 90
Put your bonnet to his right use; 'tis for the head.
Osr. I thank your lordship, it is very hot.
Ham. No, believe me, 'tis very cold; the wind is
northerly.
Osr. It is indifferent cold, my lord, indeed. 95
Ham. But yet methinks it is very sultry and hot,
    or my
complexion—

*Osr.* Exceedingly, my lord; it is very sultry, as
    'twere,—I
cannot tell how. But, my lord, his majesty bade me
signify to you that he has laid a great wager on
    your head: 100
sir, this is the matter—
*Ham.* I beseech you, remember—

                  *(Hamlet moves him to put on his hat.)*

*Osr.* Nay, good my lord; for mine ease, in good
    faith.
Sir, here is newly come to court Laertes; believe me,
    an absolute
gentleman, full of most excellent differences, of
    very 105
soft society and great showing: indeed, to speak
    feelingly of
him, he is the card or calendar of gentry, for you
    shall find
in him the continent of what part a gentleman
    would see.
*Ham.* Sir, his definement suffers no perdition
    in you;
though, I know, to divide him inventorially would
    dizzy the 110
arithmetic of memory, and yet but yaw neither, in
    respect
of his quick sail. But in the verity of extolment,
    I take
him to be a soul of great article, and his infusion
    of such
dearth and rareness, as, to make true diction of
    him, his
semblable is his mirror, and who else would trace
    him, his 115
umbrage, nothing more.
*Osr.* Your lordship speaks most infallibly of him.
*Ham.* The concernancy, sir? why do we wrap the
gentleman in our more rawer breath?
*Osr.* Sir? 120

*Hor.* Is't not possible to understand in another
   tongue?
You will do't, sir, really.
*Ham.* What imports the nomination of this
   gentleman?
*Osr.* Of Laertes?
*Hor.* His purse is empty already; all's golden
   words 125
are spent.
*Ham.* Of him, sir.
*Osr.* I know you are not ignorant—
*Ham.* I would you did, sir; yet, in faith, if you
   did, it
would not much approve me. Well, sir? 130
*Osr.* You are not ignorant of what excellence
   Laertes is—
*Ham.* I dare not confess that, lest I should compare
with him in excellence; but, to know a man well,
   were to
know himself.
*Osr.* I mean, sir, for his weapon; but in the imputa-
   tion 135
laid on him by them, in his meed he's unfellowed.
*Ham.* What's his weapon?
*Osr.* Rapier and dagger.
*Ham.* That's two of his weapons: but, well.
*Osr.* The king, sir, hath wagered with him six Barbary 140
horses: against the which he has imponed, as I take
   it, six
French rapiers and poniards, with their assigns, as
   girdle,
hanger, and so: three of the carriages, in faith,
   are very
dear to fancy, very responsive to the hilts, most
   delicate
carriages, and of very liberal conceit. 145
*Ham.* What call you the carriages?
*Hor.* I knew you must be edified by the
   margent ere
you had done.
*Osr.* The carriages, sir, are the hangers.

*HAM.* The phrase would be more germane to the 150
matter if we could carry a cannon by our sides: I
would
it might be hangers till then. But, on: six Barbary
horses
against six French swords, their assigns, and three
liberal-conceited
carriages; that's the French bet against the
Danish. Why is this 'imponed,' as you call it? 155
*OSR.* The king, sir, hath laid, sir, that in a dozen
passes between yourself and him, he shall not ex-
ceed you
three hits: he hath laid on twelve for nine; and it
would
come to immediate trial, if your lordship would
vouchsafe
the answer. 160
*HAM.* How if I answer 'no'?
*OSR.* I mean, my lord, the opposition of your
person
in trial.
*HAM.* Sir, I will walk here in the hall: if it please his
majesty, it is the breathing time of day with me; let
the 165
foils be brought, the gentleman willing, and the
king hold
his purpose, I will win for him an I can; if not, I
will gain
nothing but my shame and the odd hits.
*OSR.* Shall I redeliver you e'en so?
*HAM.* To this effect, sir, after what flourish your nature 170
will.
*OSR.* I commend my duty to your lordship.
*HAM.* Yours, yours. *(Exit Osric.)* He does well to
commend it himself; there are no tongues else for's
turn.
*HOR.* This lapwing runs away with the shell on
his 175
head.
*HAM.* He did comply with his dug before he
sucked

it. Thus has he—and many more of the same breed that
I know the drossy age dotes on—only got the tune of the
time and outward habit of encounter; a kind of yesty collection, 180
which carries them through and through the most
fond and winnowed opinions; and do but blow them to
their trial, the bubbles are out.

*(Enter a Lord)*

LORD. My lord, his majesty commended him to you by
young Osric, who brings back to him, that you attend him 185
in the hall: he sends to know if your pleasure hold to play
with Laertes, or that you will take longer time.
HAM. I am constant to my purposes; they follow the
king's pleasure: if his fitness speaks, mine is ready; now or
whensoever, provided I be so able as now. 190
LORD. The king and queen and all are coming down.
HAM. In happy time.
LORD. The queen desires you to use some gentle entertainment
to Laertes before you fall to play.
HAM. She well instructs me. *(Exit Lord.)* 195
HOR. You will lose this wager, my lord.
HAM. I do not think so; since he went into France, I
have been in continual practice; I shall win at the odds.
But thou wouldst not think how ill all's here about my
heart: but it is no matter. 200
HOR. Nay, good my lord,—
HAM. It is but foolery; but it is such a kind of gain-giving

as would perhaps trouble a woman.

*Hor.* If your mind dislike any thing, obey it. I will
forestal their repair hither, and say you are not
    fit. 205

*Ham.* Not a whit; we defy augury: there is special
providence in the fall of a sparrow. If it be now, 'tis
    not to
come; if it be not to come, it will be now; if it be
    not now,
yet it will come: the readiness is all; since no
    man has
aught of what he leaves, what is't to leave betimes?
    Let 210
be.

*(Enter KING, QUEEN, LAERTES, and Lords, OSRIC and other
Attendants with foils and gauntlets; a table and flagons of wine
on it.)*

*KING.* Come, Hamlet, come, and take this hand
    from me.

*(The King puts Laertes' hand into Hamlet's.)*

*Ham.* Give me your pardon, sir: I've done you
    wrong;
But pardon't, as you are a gentleman.
This presence knows, 215
And you must needs have heard, how I am
    punish'd
With sore distraction. What I have done,
That might your nature, honour and exception
Roughly awake, I here proclaim was madness.
Was't Hamlet wrong'd Laertes? Never Hamlet: 220
If Hamlet from himself be ta'en away,
And when he's not himself does wrong Laertes,
Then Hamlet does it not, Hamlet denies it.
Who does it then? His madness: if't be so,
Hamlet is of the faction that is wrong'd; 225
His madness is poor Hamlet's enemy.
Sir, in this audience,
Let my disclaiming from a purposed evil

Free me so far in your most generous thoughts,
That I have shot mine arrow o'er the house, 230
And hurt my brother.
LAER. I am satisfied in nature,
Whose motive, in this case, should stir me most
To my revenge: but in my terms of honour
I stand aloof, and will no reconcilement,
Till by some elder masters of known honour 235
I have a voice and precedent of peace,
To keep my name ungored. But till that time
I do receive your offer'd love like love
And will not wrong it.
HAM. I embrace it freely,
And will this brother's wager frankly play. 240
Give us the foils. Come on.
LAER. Come, one for me.
HAM. I'll be your foil, Laertes: in mine ignorance
Your skill shall, like a star i' the darkest night,
Stick fiery off indeed.
LAER. You mock me, sir.
HAM. No, by this hand. 245
KING. Give them the foils, young Osric. Cousin
Hamlet,
You know the wager?
HAM. Very well, my lord;
Your grace has laid the odds o' the weaker side.
KING. I do not fear it; I have seen you both:
But since he is better'd, we have therefore odds. 250
LAER. This is too heavy; let me see another.
HAM. This likes me well. These foils have all a
    length?

*(They prepare to play.)*

OSR. Ay, my good lord.
KING. Set me the stoups of wine upon that table.
If Hamlet give the first or second hit, 255
Or quit in answer of the third exchange,
Let all the battlements their ordnance fire;
The king shall drink to Hamlet's better breath;
And in the cup an union shall he throw,
Richer than that which four successive kings 260

In Denmark's crown have worn. Give me the cups;
And let the kettle to the trumpet speak,
The trumpet to the cannoneer without,
The cannons to the heavens, the heaven to earth,
'Now the king drinks to Hamlet.' Come, begin; 265
And you, the judges, bear a wary eye.

*Ham.* Come on, sir.

*Laer.* Come, my lord. *(They play.)*

*Ham.* One.

*Laer.* No.

*Ham.* Judgement.

*Osr.* A hit, a very palpable hit.

*Laer.* Well; again.

*King.* Stay; give me drink. Hamlet, this pearl is thine;
Here's to thy health.

*(Trumpets sound, and cannon shot off within.)*

Give him the cup. 270

*Ham.* I'll play this bout first; set it by awhile.
Come. *(They play.)* Another hit; what say you?

*Laer.* A touch, a touch, I do confess.

*King.* Our son shall win.

*Queen.* He's fat and scant of breath.
Here, Hamlet, take my napkin, rub thy brows: 275
The queen carouses to thy fortune, Hamlet.

*Ham.* Good madam!

*King.* Gertrude, do not drink.

*Queen.* I will, my lord; I pray you, pardon me.

*King.* *(Aside)* It is the poison'd cup; it is too late.

*Ham.* I dare not drink yet, madam; by and by. 280

*Queen.* Come, let me wipe thy face.

*Laer.* My lord, I'll hit him now.

*King.* I do not think't.

*Laer.* *(Aside)* And yet it is almost against my conscience.

*Ham.* Come, for the third, Laertes: you but dally;
I pray you, pass with your best violence; 285
I am afeard you make a wanton of me.

*Laer.* Say you so? come on. *(They play.)*

*Osr.* Nothing, neither way.

*Laer.* Have at you now!

*(Laertes wounds Hamlet; then, in scuffling, they change rapiers, and Hamlet wounds Laertes.)*

*King.* Part them; they are incensed.
*Ham.* Nay, come, again. *(The Queen falls.)*
*Osr.* Look to the queen there, ho! 290
*Hor.* They bleed on both sides. How is it, my lord?
*Osr.* How is 't, Laertes?
*Laer.* Why, as a woodcock to mine own springe,
   Osric;
I am justly kill'd with mine own treachery.
*Ham.* How does the queen?
*King.* She swounds to see them bleed. 295
*Queen.* No, no, the drink, the drink,—O my dear
   Hamlet,—
The drink, the drink! I am poison'd. *(Dies.)*
*Ham.* O villany! Ho! let the door be lock'd:
Treachery! seek it out.
*Laer.* It is here, Hamlet: Hamlet, thou art slain; 300
No medicine in the world can do thee good,
In thee there is not half an hour of life;
The treacherous instrument is in thy hand,
Unbated and envenom'd: the foul practice
Hath turn'd itself on me; lo, here I lie, 305
Never to rise again: thy mother's poison'd:
I can no more: the king, the king's to blame.
*Ham.* The point envenom'd too!
Then, venom, to thy work. *(Stabs the King.)*
*All.* Treason! treason! 310
*King.* O, yet defend me, friends; I am but hurt.
*Ham.* Here, thou incestuous, murderous, damned
   Dane,
Drink off this potion: is thy union here?
Follow my mother. *(King dies.)*
*Laer.* He is justly served;
It is a poison temper'd by himself. 315
Exchange forgiveness with me, noble Hamlet:
Mine and my father's death come not upon thee,
Nor thine on me! *(Dies.)*
*Ham.* Heaven make thee free of it! I follow thee.

I am dead, Horatio. Wretched queen, adieu! 320
You that look pale and tremble at this chance,
That are but mutes or audience to this act,
Had I but time—as this fell sergeant, death,
Is strict in his arrest—O, I could tell you—
But let it be. Horatio, I am dead; 325
Thou livest; report me and my cause aright
To the unsatisfied.
*Hor.* Never believe it:
I am more an antique Roman than a Dane:
Here's yet some liquor left.
*Ham.* As thou'rt a man,
Give me the cup: let go; by heaven, I'll have't. 330
O good Horatio, what a wounded name,
Things standing thus unknown, shall live
    behind me!
If thou didst ever hold me in thy heart,
Absent thee from felicity awhile,
And in this harsh world draw thy breath in
    pain, 335
*To tell my story. (March afar off, and shot within.)*
What warlike noise is this?
*Osr.* Young Fortinbras, with conquest come from
    Poland,
To the ambassadors of England gives
This warlike volley.
*Ham.* O, I die, Horatio;
The potent poison quite o'er-crows my spirit: 340
I cannot live to hear the news from England;
But I do prophesy the election lights
On Fortinbras: he has my dying voice;
So tell him, with the occurrents, more and less,
Which have solicited. The rest is silence. *(Dies.)* 345
*Hor.* Now cracks a noble heart. Good night, sweet
    prince,
And flights of angels sing thee to thy rest! *(March
    within.)*
Why does the drum come hither?

*(Enter Fortinbras, and the English Ambassadors, with drum,
    colours, and Attendants.)*

*Fort.* Where is this sight?

*Hor.* What is it you would see?

If aught of woe or wonder, cease your search. 350

*Fort.* This quarry cries on havoc. O proud death,

What feast is toward in thine eternal cell,

That thou so many princes at a shot

So bloodily hast struck?

*First Amb.* The sight is dismal;

And our affairs from England come too late: 355

The ears are senseless that should give us hearing.

To tell him his commandment is fulfill'd,

That Rosencrantz and Guildenstern are dead:

Where should we have our thanks?

*Hor.* Not from his mouth

Had it the ability of life to thank you: 360

He never gave commandment for their death.

But since, so jump upon this bloody question,

You from the Polack wars, and you from England,

Are here arrived, give order that these bodies

High on a stage be placed to the view; 365

And let me speak to the yet unknowing world

How these things came about: so shall you hear

Of carnal, bloody and unnatural acts,

Of accidental judgements, casual slaughters,

Of deaths put on by cunning and forced cause, 370

And, in this upshot, purposes mistook

Fall'n on the inventors' heads: all this can I

Truly deliver.

*Fort.* Let us haste to hear it,

And call the noblest to the audience.

For me, with sorrow I embrace my fortune: 375

I have some rights of memory in this kingdom,

Which now to claim my vantage doth invite me.

*Hor.* Of that I shall have also cause to speak,

And from his mouth whose voice will draw on
    more:

But let this same be presently perform'd, 380

Even while men's minds are wild; lest more
    mischance

On plots and errors happen.

*Fort.* Let four captains

Bear Hamlet, like a soldier, to the stage;

For he was likely, had he been put on,
To have proved most royally: and, for his passage,

385
The soldiers' music and the rites of war
Speak loudly for him.
Take up the bodies: such a sight as this
Becomes the field, but here shows much amiss.
Go, bid the soldiers shoot. 390

*(A dead march. Exeunt, bearing off the bodies: after which a peal of ordnance is shot off.)*